# Industrial Internet

Center for Electronics and Information Studies,
Chinese Academy of Engineering

# Industrial Internet

Research on the Development of Electronic
Information Engineering Technology
in China

Center for Electronics and Information Studies
Chinese Academy of Engineering
Beijing, China

ISBN 978-981-15-7489-4      ISBN 978-981-15-7490-0   (eBook)
https://doi.org/10.1007/978-981-15-7490-0

This Springer imprint is published by the registered company Springer Nature Singapore Pte Ltd.
The registered company address is: 152 Beach Road, #21-01/04 Gateway East, Singapore 189721,
Singapore

# Preface

## The *Research on the Development of Electronic Information Engineering Technology in China* **Book Series**

In today's world, the wave of information technologies featured by digitalization, networking, and intelligence is gaining momentum. Information technologies are experiencing rapid changes with each passing day and are fully applied in production and life, bringing about profound changes in global economic, political, and security landscapes. Among diverse information technologies, electronic information engineering technology is one of the most innovative and widely used technologies, and plays its greatest role in driving the development of other S&T fields. It is not only a field of intense competition in technological innovation, but also an important strategic direction for key players to fuel economic growth and seek competitive advantages over other players. Electronic information engineering technology is a typical "enabling technology" that enables technological progress in almost all other fields. Its integration with biotechnology, new energy technology, and new material technology is expected to set off a new round of technological revolution and industrial transformation, thereby bringing about new opportunities for the evolution of human society. Electronic information is a typical "engineering technology" and one of the most straightforward and practical tools. It realizes direct and close integration of scientific discoveries and technological innovations with industrial developments, greatly speeding up technological progress. Hence, it is regarded as a powerful force to change the world. Electronic information engineering technology is a vital driving force of China's rapid economic and social development in the past seven decades, especially in the past four decades of reform and opening up. Looking ahead, advances and innovations in electronic information engineering technology will remain to be one of the most important engines driving human progress.

CAE is China's foremost academic and advisory institution in engineering and technological sciences. Guided by the general development trends of science and technology around the world, CAE is committed to providing scientific, forward-looking, and timely advice for innovation-driven scientific and technological progress from a strategic and long-term perspective. CAE's mission is to function as a national high-end think tank. To fulfill the mission, the Division of Information and Electronic Engineering, under the guidance of its Vice President Zuoning Chen, Director Xicheng Lu, and the Standing Committee, mobilized more than 300 academicians and experts to jointly compile the General Section and the Special Section of this book (hereinafter referred to as the "Blue Book"). The first stage of compilation was headed by Academicians Jiangxing Wu and Manqing Wu (from the end of 2015 to June 2018), and the second one was headed by Academicians Shaohua Yu and Jun Lu (since September 2018). The purposes of compiling the Blue Book are as follows:

By analyzing technological progress and introducing major breakthroughs and marked achievements made in the electronic information field both at home and abroad each year, to provide reference for China's scientific and technical personnel to accurately grasp the development trend of the field and provide support for China's policymakers to formulate related development strategies.

The "Blue Book" is compiled according to the following principles:

1. **Ensure appropriate description of annual increment.** The field of electronic information engineering technology enjoys a broad coverage and high development speed. Thus, the General Section should ensure an appropriate description of the annual increment, which is about the recent progress, new characteristics, and new trends.
2. **Selection of hot points and highlight points.** China's technological development is still at a mixed stage where it needs to assume the role of follower, contender, and leader simultaneously. Hence, the Special Themes should seek to depict the developmental characteristics the industry focuses on, and should center on the "hot points" and "highlight points" along the development journey.
3. **Integration of General Section and Special Section.** The program consists of two sections: the General section and the Special Themes. The former adopts a macro perspective to discuss the global and Chinese development of electronic information engineering technology, and its outlook; the latter provides detailed descriptions of hot points and highlight points in the 13 subfields.

## Application System

8. Underwater acoustic engineering

13. Computer application

| **Acquiring Perception** | **Computation and Control** | **Cyber Security** |
|---|---|---|
| 3. Perception | 10. Control | 6. Network and communication |
| 5. Electromagnetic space | 11. Cognition | 7. Cybersecurity |
| | 12. Computer systems and software | |

## Common Basis

1. Microelectronic and Optoelectronics    2. Optical engineering

4. Measurement/Metrology and Instruments

9. Electromagnetic field and electromagnetic environment effect

Classification Diagrams of 13 Subfields of information and electronic engineering technology

The above graphic displays 5 categories and 13 subcategories, or special themes that bear distinct granularity. However, every subfield is closely connected with each other in terms of technological correlations, which allows easier matching with their corresponding disciplines.

Currently, the compilation of the "Blue Book" is still at a trial stage where careless omissions are unavoidable. Hence, we welcome comments and corrections.

## The Special Theme *Industrial Internet* in *Research on the Development of Electronic Information Engineering Technology in China* Book Series

One year ago, the State Council released the *Guidance on Deepening the "Internet plus Advanced Manufacturing Industry" and Developing the Industrial Internet*. Since then, governments at all levels, manufacturing companies, automation companies, ICT companies, internet companies, research institutes, and other parties actively participate in the construction and promotion of the Industrial Internet. To display the phased progress of the Industrial Internet, industrial practices, and results in key industries, the core competencies and solutions of the Industrial Internet, and to clarify the innovation & development trend and direction in the future and other major aspects that have been widely concerned, *Research on the Development of*

*Electronic Information Engineering Technology in China* has investigated current developments of the Industrial Internet, collected and analyzed the latest progress and materials of it and compiled the *Special Section of Industrial Internet*. By doing so, it hopes to provide some references and guidance to participating entities from the political, production, education, research and application fields, facilitate the conclusion of industrial consensus, and promote the rapid and healthy development of the Industrial Internet.

This book starts with the birth background of the Industrial Internet, clarifying its definition, contents, and architecture; following that is a review of its development trends in China and across the world, mainly in terms of policies, networks, platforms, security, application, and standards. It finishes up with information about the integration of Industrial Internet with a series of new-generation information technologies, such as the Time Sensitive Networking, 5G, Edge Computing, Blockchain, and Artificial Intelligence. It will provide reference for studying the future trend of innovation.

This book is intended for researchers and industrial staffs who have been following the current situation and future trends of the Industrial Internet. Meanwhile, it also bears high value of reference for experts, scholars, and technical and engineering managers of different levels and different fields.

This book is divided into five chapters. Chapter 1 proposes the architecture and major elements of the Industrial Internet, and clarifies its definition and functions. Chapters 2 and 3 introduce its current progresses both at home and abroad in terms of policy measures, technological systems, industrial ecologies, and application modes. Chapter 4 discusses the potential trend of innovation and development in this field, in a bid to explore a path for large-scale application and practices. Chapter 5 is about summary and acknowledgment.

When compiling this book, we have received broad and strong supports from both Chinese and foreign enterprises. They have not only provided massive materials about their solutions and results that are based on their own development situations but also proactively helped us organize field surveys and seminars, which has greatly contributed to the formation and implementation of opinions in this book.

The Industrial Internet is a long-term development and evolution process. Considering that, we will continue with in-depth studies, and revise and update this book with new findings on a timely basis, taking into account the industrial feedback and development situations both in China and abroad.

Beijing, China                                        Center for Electronics and Information Studies,
                                                             Chinese Academy of Engineering

# List of Series Contributors

The guidance group and working group of *Research on the Development of Electronic Information Engineering Technology in China* series are as follows:

**Guidance Group**

    **Leader:** Zuoning Chen, Xichen Lu

    **Member** (In alphabetical order):

Aiguo Fei, Baoyan Duan, Binxing Fang, Bohu Li, Changxiang Shen, Cheng Wu, Chengjun Wang, Chun Chen, Desen Yang, Dianyuan Fang, Endong Wang, Guangjun Zhang, Guangnan Ni, Guofan Jin, Guojie Li, Hao Dai, Hequan Wu, Huilin Jiang, Huixing Gong, Jiangxing Wu, Jianping Wu, Jiaxiong Fang, Jie Chen, Jiubin Tan, Jun Lu, Lianghui Chen, Manqing Wu, Qinping Zhao, Qionghai Dai, Shanghe Liu, Shaohua Yu, Tianchu Li, Tianran Wang, Tianyou Chai, Wen Gao, Wenhua Ding, Yu Wei, Yuanliang Ma, Yueguang Lv, Yueming Li, Zejin Liu, Zhijie Chen, Zhonghan Deng, Zhongqi Gao, Zishen Zhao, Zuyan Xu

**Working Group**

    **Leader:** Shaohua Yu, Jun Lu

    **Deputy Leader:** Da An, Meimei Dang, Shouren Xu

    **Member** (In alphabetical order):

Denian Shi, Dingyi Zhang, Fangfang Dai, Fei Dai, Fei Xing, Feng Zhou, Gang Qiao, Lan Zhou, Li Tao, Liang Chen, Lun Li, Mo Liu, Nan Meng, Peng Wang, Qiang Fu, Qingguo Wang, Rui Zhang, Shaohui Li, Wei He, Wei Xie, Xiangyang Ji, Xiaofeng Hu, Xingquan Zhang, Xiumei Shao, Yan Lu, Ying Wu, Yue Lu, Yunfeng Wei, Yuxiang Shu, Zheng Zheng, Zhigang Shang, Zhuang Liu

# About the Authors

Chinese Academy of Engineering (CAE) is China's foremost academic and advisory institution in engineering and technological sciences, which has been enrolled in the first batch of pilot national high-end think tanks. As a national institution, CAE's missions are to study major strategic issues in economic and social development as well as in engineering technology progress, and to build itself into a S&T think tank having significant influences on decision-making of national strategic issues. In today's world, the wave of information technologies featured by digitalization, networking, and intelligence is gaining momentum. Information technologies are experiencing rapid changes with each passing day and are fully applied in production and life, bringing about profound changes in global economic, political, and security landscapes. Among diverse information technologies, electronic information engineering technology is one of the most innovative and widely used technologies, and plays its greatest role in driving the development of other S&T fields. In order to better carry out strategic studies on electronic information engineering technology, promote innovation in relevant systems and mechanisms and integrate superior resources, Center for Electronics and Information Studies (hereinafter referred to the "Center") was established in November 2015 by CAE in collaboration with Cyberspace Administration of China (CAC), the Ministry of Industry and Information Technology (MIIT), and China Electronics Technology Group Corporation (CETC).

The Center pursues high-level, open, and prospective development, and is committed to conducting theoretical and application-oriented researches on crosscutting, overarching, and strategically important hot topics concerning electronic information engineering technologies, and providing consultancy services for policymaking by brainstorming ideas from CAE academicians and experts and scholars from national ministries and commissions, businesses, public institutions, universities, and research institutions. The Center's mission is to build a top-notch strategic think tank that provides scientific, forward-looking, and timely advice for national policymaking in terms of electronic information engineering technology.

The main authors of *Industrial Internet* are Xiaohui Yu, Haihua Li, Shaohua Yu, Xinyi Wang, Xinhao Jiang, Hengsheng Zhang, Yang Liu, Xiaoman Liu, Song Luo, and Nian Sun.

# Acknowledgments

We are thankful to Academician Hequan Wu for his review and approval of the book and for his valuable advice on the book. This book was written with the guidance and assistance from numerous experts, and Ying Huang, Yihui Zhang, Jiadong Du, Difei Liu, Lin Yuan, Denian Shi, Rongmei Xiao, Mo Liu, Huirong Tian, Kai Wei, and Zhibo Qi from the China Academy of Information and Communications Technology took part in the compilation of some parts of the book. We acknowledge their contribution to this book.

# Contents

# Chapter 1
# Introduction

## 1.1 Background of the Industrial Internet

At present, the innovative development of the Internet and the new industrial revolution are in a period of historical confluence, and Internet applications are penetrating and spreading from the consumption link to the manufacturing link [1, 2]. Meanwhile, following the economic crisis, in order for the revival of the domestic manufacturing sector, further maintenance of their global leadership and the development of a new blue ocean, respectively, governments, industrial magnates and information & communications businesses have been jointly promoting the rise of the Industrial Internet.

In 2012, General Electric (GE), a U.S. high-end manufacturing giant, first put forward the development of the Industrial Internet globally. GE built an Industrial Internet platform through deep application of new generation information technologies such as cloud computing, Internet of Things (IoT) and big data, and offered such platform-based intelligent services, with an attempt to reshape the industrial growth model, to occupy new commanding heights of the industry and to consolidate its global leadership. In 2014, GE, together with Cisco, IBM, Intel and AT&T, founded the Industrial Internet Consortium (IIC), speeding up the popularization of the concept, project implementation and industrial cooperation in respect of the Internet Industrial throughout the world. As of December 2018, IIC already had more than 260 corporate members from over 30 countries and regions, including traditional manufacturers such as GE and Siemens, software enterprises such as SAP and Dassault, as well as traditional information & communications enterprises such as Huawei, Microsoft and AT&T. Moreover, IIC has had over 50 enterprises from different countries jointly facilitate the work concerning test beds, and has successively entered into cooperation with governments or industrial organizations from such countries as Germany, Japan, Russia, Brazil, France and India. Also, IIC has established contact-letter relations with more than 20 standardization bodies all over the world, including Institute of Electric and Electronic Engineers (IEEE),

© China Science Publishing & Media Ltd (Science Press) 2020
Chinese Academy of Engineering, *Industrial Internet*,
https://doi.org/10.1007/978-981-15-7490-0_1

International Standardization Organization (ISO) and International Electrotechnical Commission (IEC), for cooperation in the research on technologies, requirements, standards and so forth. Currently, IIC has become an important international organization promoting the development of the Industrial Internet worldwide [3].

## 1.2  Concept of the Industrial Internet

Industrial Internet is a key infrastructure, new-type application model and brand-new industrial ecosystem [4, 5] amid deep integration of new generation information & communications technologies and industrial economy, as is shown in Fig. 1.1. It has a profound impact on the mode of production, management and service in the traditional industry, serves as a catalyst for innovations and changes in technologies, models, business forms, and industries, and is becoming the new cornerstone of a prosperous digital economy. For China, the Industrial Internet is a new approach to the participation in the international network governance and a new tool to coordinate the national manufacturing and cyber development strategy [5].

Industrial Internet is more than a simple application of the Internet in industries, but has multiple features. Firstly, it is the fundamentality. Industrial Internet is a key infrastructure propping up intelligent upgrading of the industry as it has built a new network consisting of factory internal and external networks, and established an Industrial Internet platform connecting all industrial factors and serving optimal allocation of resources. Second is the penetrability. Industrial Internet can not only be applied in the manufacturing sectors, but also extend to all sectors of the real economy, thus providing basic support for network-based and intelligent upgrading of different industries and then promoting the transformation and upgrading of the real economy.

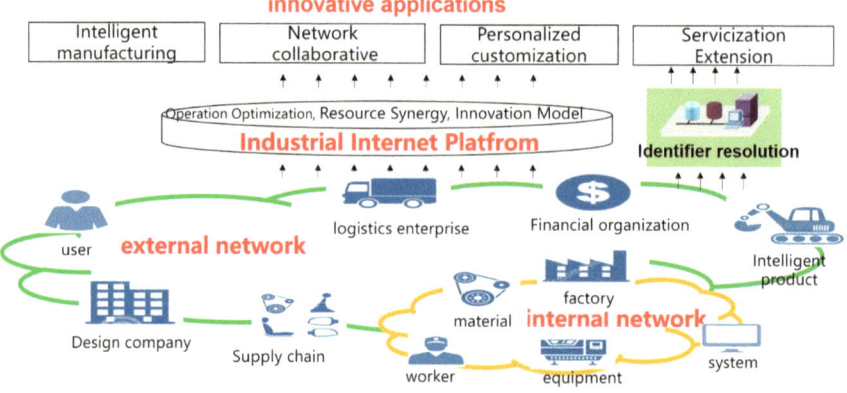

**Fig. 1.1**  Diagram of the industrial internet

## 1.3 Architecture of the Industrial Internet

The core of the Industrial Internet is to form data-driven intelligence based on comprehensive interconnection, with network, data and security being the basic elements of the Industrial Internet, as is shown in Fig. 1.2.

From the function system perspective, the Industrial Internet includes three major systems: network, platform and security. Among them, network is the foundation, platform is the core, and security is the guarantee [3, 5], as is shown in Fig. 1.3.

The network system is the foundation of ubiquitous deep interconnection of industrial processes and links, and includes internetworking, identifier resolution and information exchange. By building low-latency, highly reliable and widely covering network infrastructure, seamless transfer of information and data can be achieved between different production links and factors, thereby underpinning the formation of a mode of production that enables real-time perception, synergetic interaction and intelligent feedback.

The platform system is a hub connecting all industrial factors and also the core of industrial resource allocation. It connected with both devices and applications, drives the standardized, software-based, modularized and service-oriented development of manufacturing capacity and industrial knowledge through mass data aggregation, modeling analysis and application development, thus supporting the upgrading of

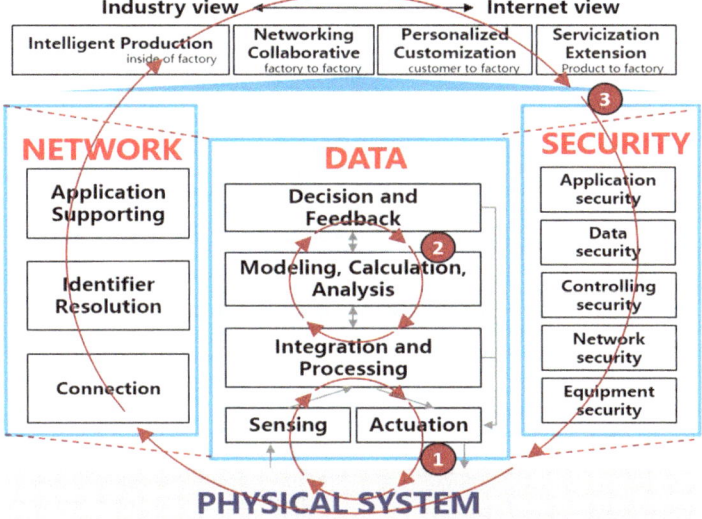

**Fig. 1.2** Basic elements of the industrial internet (above "Network security" should be "Cyber security")

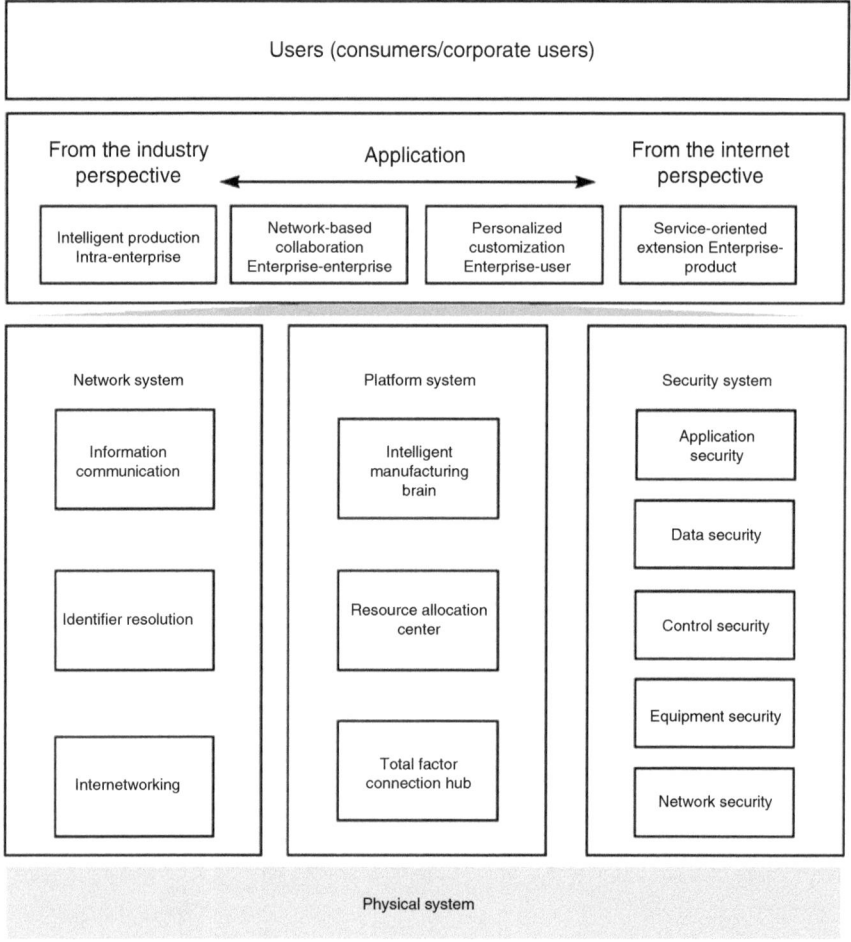

**Fig. 1.3** Systems constituting the industrial internet (above "Network security" should be "Cyber security")

the mode of industrial production, business model innovation and efficient resource allocation, and lies at the core of building a new manufacturing ecosystem [6].

The security system provides guarantee for healthy and orderly development of the Industrial Internet and covers security at five levels, such as device, control, network, application and data [4, 5]. The establishment of a security system for the Industrial Internet can help preserve factory internal and external network facilities, protect industrial intelligent devices and systems from internal and external attacks, ensure reliable operation of Industrial Internet platforms and their application, lower the risk of industrial data leakage and tampering, and realize all-round protection of the Industrial Internet.

# Chapter 2
# Global Development Trend

## 2.1 Policies and Measures of Major Countries

In recent years, the Industrial Internet has gradually become an important tool whereby countries in the world promote digital, network-based and intelligent development of manufacturing. Governments have been energetically pushing forward the development of the Industrial Internet at home through strategic guidance, financial support, creation of a more favorable environment and other means, thus occupying commanding heights of the wider-range and deeper-level technology revolution and industrial transformation [7].

**In the U.S., the development of the Industrial Internet is to a large extent spontaneously driven by the industrial circle itself, though the government still plays a key role.** Firstly, the U.S. has strengthened strategic guidance. On October 5, 2018, the National Science and Technology Council released the "Strategy for American Leadership in Advanced Manufacturing" as an update of the National Strategic Plan for Advanced Manufacturing, which strategy underscores the need to actively promote digital and intelligent development of manufacturing. In February 2019, the White House released its plan for future industrial development, which proposes to increase investment in advanced manufacturing-related key areas by revising existing laws and other means. Secondly, the U.S. guarantees financial support. The National Science Foundation (NSF) has launched the Cyber-Physical Systems (CPS) program since 2006, and CPS is one of the important technologies underlying the development of the Industrial Internet. In 2019, the Networking and Information Technology Research and Development (NITRD) offered an accumulated fund of USD 139 million to support the R&D and transformation of the CPS technology. Thirdly, the U.S. is committed to cultivating actors of innovation. In 2014, the United States Department of Defense led the establishment of the Digital Manufacturing and Design Innovation Institute (DMDII), whose core members include corporate giants such as GE, Lockheed Martin, Rolls-Royce and Siemens. Focusing on four major areas, namely advanced manufacturing, intelligent machine,

© China Science Publishing & Media Ltd (Science Press) 2020
Chinese Academy of Engineering, *Industrial Internet*,
https://doi.org/10.1007/978-981-15-7490-0_2

advanced analysis and cyber-physical security, DMDII is engaged in the R&D of technologies, validation of standards and training of personnel with respect to the Industrial Internet, and use of Industrial Internet-related technologies to reduce production and time costs in the design and manufacturing of complicated products by relevant enterprises. In February 2018, DMDII released the Strategic Investment Plan 2018, guiding investments mainly to areas such as design, future factory, supply chain and cyber security in 2018, with all tasks and objectives covering core elements including network, data and security. The construction of the DMDII has spread and lowered risks facing enterprises in their deployment and implementation of Industrial Internet solutions and can help enterprises stride over the "valley of death". Meanwhile, DMDII is integrated with regional economic clusters, creating and drawing closer partnerships between enterprises in the region and pushing for regional cluster development [8, 9]. In February 2019, the United States Department of Defense invested USD ten million to support DMDII's transformation into an independent organization mainly studying technologies and products regarding Internet connection.

**In Germany, both federal and local governments are accelerating the implementation of the Industry 4.0 Strategy by taking multiple measures in respect of policy, financial, personnel and others at the same time.** Firstly, they have perfected the top-level design. In order to fully tap the potentials of information technology (IT) in promoting industrial development and seize opportunities brought by the new industrial revolution as early as possible. The German government has issued a series of policies and measures to support and guide the development of Industry 4.0, successively facilitated improvements in institutions related to Industry 4.0 in 2012, 2014 and 2016, and released series strategy and policy guides to ensure effective deployment and implementation of Industry 4.0, thus providing strong policy guarantee for continuous advancement and system construction of Industry 4.0. Secondly, they have enhanced financial support. German Ministry of Education and Research (Bundesministerium für Bildung und Forchung, BMBF) has allocated totally more than hundreds of millions of Euros to fund the Industry 4.0 program. German Federal Ministry of Economic Affairs and Energy (Bundesministerium für Wirtschaft und Energie, BMWi) plans to invest EUR 50 million to support the research in respect of Industry 4.0, including projects on legislation, IT security, future labor conditions and skills, and standardization. The German government mainly supports small and medium-sized enterprises (SMEs) in the development of the Industrial Internet. BMWi will invest EUR 56 million in building 10 (12 as planned) digital capital centers for SMEs under the initiative "© (SME) 4.0—Digital Production and Work Processes", so as to solve cost and security problems for SMEs in the process of digitalization and introduction of Industry 4.0 [10]. The High-Tech Strategy 2025 released by Germany in 2018 states that over EUR 15 billion will be invested to carry forward the development of seven key areas, including Industry 4.0. Thirdly, they have intensified organizational guarantee. Germany has established three application promotion platforms, such as Plattform Industrie 4.0, Labs Network Industrie 4.0 (LNI4.0) and Standardization Council Industrie 4.0, allowed full play to the role of the government, industries and enterprises to create synergy, thus expediting the development of technologies, standards and industries in connection with Industry 4.0 [11].

**In Japan, multi-dimensional coordinated arrangements have been made to advance the Industrial Internet and social changes.** Firstly, Japan has enhanced financial support. Japan increased investment in Industrial Internet-related areas, and put forward the "Connected Industries" initiative, which is intended to pool government funds to address weaknesses and bottlenecks in industrial development and guide stakeholders to actively take part in the development of the Industrial Internet industry. In June 2017, Japan adopted the basic policy for economic and fiscal operations of 2017 and a new strategy for economic growth titled "Future Investment Strategy", which identifies investment in human resources as the backbone and construction of the IoT and application of artificial intelligence (AI) as two priorities. The "Future Investment Strategy" makes it clear that Japan will support the development in five major fields, such as infrastructure, financial services and supply chain, through a variety of policies, and actively promote extensive application of the technological change represented by AI and the IoT in all sectors of production and life on the premise of addressing existing problems, so as to achieve the ultimate goal of "Society 5.0" [12]. Secondly, Japan has built an industrial ecosystem. The Japanese government encourages the establishment of industry alliances and similar organizations focusing on manufacturing, with a view to advancing the development of the Industrial Internet through industry-university-research-application cooperation. In June 2015, 23 Japanese enterprises initiated the Industrial Value Chain Initiative (IVI) alliance, aiming at establishing a mechanism that enables combination of the expertise of different enterprises by distinguishing areas of cooperation and competition, sharing enterprises' reference models and other means, and then attaining relevant policy goals. In October 2015, with the guidance from Japan's Ministry of Internal Affairs and Communications and Ministry of Economy, Trade and Industry (METI), a number of enterprises from home and abroad made up the "IoT Acceleration Consortium" [13], under which there is an IoT promotion laboratory that develops and promotes in society as early as possible advanced IoT projects, whilst helping matching and cooperation between solutions in different fields. Thirdly, Japan has propelled international cooperation. The Japanese government encourages and guides its industrial circle to actively participate in international cooperation, thus boosting the integration of its industries into the global industrial ecosystem. At the government level, Japan has been vigorously driving strategic alignment with Germany and France and has signed documents on cooperation with relevant countries in key areas. At the industry level, Japan encourages its industrial circle represented by the IVI to actively seek cooperation all over the world, thereby aggressively integrating the Japanese industrial circle into the global Industrial Internet ecosystem.

Beyond these, European countries such as the UK and France, and emerging economies like India have in succession identified the Industrial Internet as a national development strategy for promoting technology innovation, pushing forward intelligent industrial development and achieving integration and reengineering of industrial processes in the next 5 to 10 years, and carried out strategic deployment in advance [14].

## 2.2   Network

**The application of new-type network technology has become a global hotspot.**
Time Sensitive Network (TSN), as a new technology to meet the demands of high-speed, highly-reliable and highly-real-time Internet connection in factories, has attracted high attentions of the industrial circle. In HANNOVER MESSE 2018, Siemens, Huawei and IIC released their TSN products, solutions and test beds. Edge computing is accelerating comprehensively. American open fog computing alliance Openfog has been merged with IIC to better drive deployment of edge computing in the industrial Internet; Edgecross Consortium, a major corporate organization of Japan, has sped up the deployment and development of edging computing technology and product; industrial enterprises such as GE and Siemens, and communication enterprises including Cisco, Microsoft and Amazon, have all released relevant products. Studies on the application of 5G in industrial field has been on the fast track, and Ericsson, Huawei and Vodafone, together with Bosch, Siemens and Yokogawa, have established the 5G alliance of industrial internet and automation (5G-ACIA), to move ahead with industrial application of 5G. The technology of software-defined network (SDN) has gone deep into industrial production scenarios gradually, and German Fraunhofer IZM and some German enterprises are working to give impetus to application of SDN in industry.

**The technology of identifier resolution is still in its early days and the application keeps deepening.** Currently, there are various identifier coding and resolution technologies in the world, which can be classified into two routes for technical development. One is the technical improvement route, which mainly relies on the current Internet domain name system for improvement; the other is the technical change route, with the Handle identifier resolution system invented by Dr. Robert Kahn, father of Internet, as one of the typical solutions. In the future, new technical solutions may appear. In some countries, the industrial Internet identifier resolution system has realized initial application in the manufacturing industry, and smart factories based on the identifier resolution technology have come into being. In view of relevant deployment and application effects in the U.S. and France, there exist some critical problems to be solved in terms of industrial application of the identifier resolution system, of which, some problems are beyond common system design, including those of safety, elastic system, integratability, interoperability, combinability, data management and intelligent system, and the combination with cutting-edge technologies of AI, blockchain and big data has become the significant direction to address such problems. Due to the diversity of industrial application requirements, there are some uncertainties in the direction of the future technical standards for identifier, and the final result of which kind of technical standard will win out or that multiple technical standards will co-exist is still to be tested by the practice.

## 2.3   Platform

**Industrial Internet platforms focus on service capacity requirements and continue to strengthen their key technologies.** In the first place, edge technologies and platforms have completed integrated application, facilitating integration of cutting-edge technologies such as big data and AI into terminal devices. For instance, Microsoft has completed the transition of its business logic to edge devices with the aid of the edge platform Azure IoT Edge [15]. Secondly, new network technologies assist these platforms with wider-range and cheaper device interconnection. For example, in order to meet lower power consumption and other demands, Cisco has introduced the Jasper Control Center, which can support the narrow band Internet of Things (NB-IoT) to realize automation and real-time data analysis in case of mass devices. Thirdly, these platforms focus on data analysis and the application of digital twin modeling to consolidate the foundation of intelligent application in an all-round manner. For example, Parametric Technology Corporation (PTC) has successfully imported and integrated external data analysis tools by using Analytics Manager in the ThingWorx platform. Siemens has integrated product data in the MindSphere platform and built digital twins through big data to optimize product design. Fourthly, the platforms have accelerated the layout for the low-code development technology to lower the threshold and time cost for platform application innovation. An example is that Siemens has introduced the low-code development technology owned by Medix, which has been acquired by Siemens, into the MindSphere platform, so as to comprehensively shorten the cycle of innovations in industrial APPs [16].

**Industry magnates have all quickened their arrangements for Industrial Internet platforms.** First of all, they attach an increasing importance to platform-related services [17]. With digital industries as one of its core businesses, relevant revenues of Siemens registered over EUR 14 billion in 2017. ABB has advanced the transformation of industrial digital solutions in the four leading businesses based on its Ability platform. Secondly, they continue to increase platform-related inputs. By summarizing experience in application, Siemens has upgraded its MindSphere platform to Version 3.0, further improving platform functions and performance [18]. Emerson Electric has improved the service capacity of its platform in the field of pneumatics by acquiring the Germany-based company Aventics. Finally, they have been facilitating the application and deployment of platforms in different industries. Microsoft's Azure IoT platform has unveiled industrial solutions such as connected factory and predictive maintenance, and on this basis, worked with the UK-based company Rolls-Royce for joint research and development of a remote operation and maintenance system for aircraft engines. Through the deployment of more than 480,000 installation sites worldwide, Schneider Electric's EcoStruxure platform has gathered more than 20,000 developers and system integrators in its ecosystem, and managed over 1.6 million pieces of assets [19].

**Start-ups are becoming a new force driving platform development.** On the one hand, more and more technological innovation-based enterprises begin to dabble in the field of Industrial Internet platforms. For instance, the U.S.-based Sight Machine has continuously accumulated knowledge on product quality control and production line process management in its platform to serve business expansion. On the other hand, the capital market is increasingly leaning to platform start-ups with outstanding performance. Since its establishment, Uptake, a U.S.-based company, has financed more than USD 250 million in total, with an estimated market value of up to USD 2.3 billion [20].

**Cross-industry cooperation focusing on Industrial Internet platforms is active and the ecological development of platforms is increasingly deepening.** Firstly, different platform enterprises cooperate to complement each other, thus bringing down their R&D costs. For example, GE and Siemens, respectively, have entered into cooperation with Microsoft and AliCloud in renting low-cost cloud infrastructure resources, not only relieving their input pressure, but also improving underlying performance. Secondly, cross-industry cooperation can help accumulate specialized knowledge and then improve the supply of platform solutions. For example, Schneider's EcoStruxure platform has maintained deep cooperation with industrial system integrators to acquire knowledge in various industries and form industrial APPs and solutions oriented towards different scenarios. Thirdly, through capital cooperation, industries make concerted efforts to push the development of platforms. For example, Rockwell and PTC join hands through a USD one billion equity investment to improve their competitiveness in the field of platforms in all aspects through business complementation.

Moreover, a platform-oriented ecological cooperation mechanism is taking shape at a quick pace: Siemens is building the "MindSphere World" together with various enterprises to improve platforms' ecosystem construction and promotion capabilities [21].

## 2.4 Security

**There has been a lot of practical exploration into Industrial Internet security**, covering five areas such as device security, control security, cyber security, platform security and data security. In terms of device security, in order for strong identity authentication of Industrial Internet devices, currently measures such as reinforcing operating systems and issuing certificates have been taken, ensuring authentic and trustworthy device identities at the chip level. Typical examples include two solutions to device security, namely Symantec's Critical System Protection and Symantec Device Certificate Service, which have issued over one billion security certificates to connected devices worldwide, covering a wide range of fields such as intelligent instrument, cable box and modem. In terms of control security, given the uniqueness of the control systems in the Industrial Internet, auditing of industrial control system behaviors is subject to specific requirements. The deployment is made in a way that control systems in the Industrial Internet are audited through mirroring monitoring while ensuring that monitoring network cards cannot actively send out data packages. In terms of cyber security, the strategy of overall cyber security defense in depth has been adopted to strengthen the security defense of Industrial Internet networks in all dimensions. In terms of platform security, on the basis of the actual conditions of platform architectures, a combination of hardware reinforcement, boundary isolation, security audit, access control, behavior control, risk tracking and other technologies has been used to accelerate the improvement of the security protection capacity of Industrial Internet platforms, with a view to improving the overall capacity. In terms of data security, full life cycle of data has been covered and data encryption and data security audit have been made full use of to guarantee data security.

For example, Siemens has established a strategic partnership with the U.S.-based company Identify3D (ID3D) to comprehensively improve data security clearance and encryption and fully ensure data integrity in all links and processes throughout the value chain through end-to-end data security solutions [22].

**The market size of global Industrial Internet security products is growing year by year and the industrial pattern is gradually improving.** Industrial security protection products mainly include industrial firewalls, intrusion detection and protection systems, and industrial security gateways; industrial security management products focus on access control and terminal security management; industrial security compliance products, such as security baseline management, security testing and evaluation and other tools, remain a blank in the market. From the market application perspective, Industrial Internet security products are highly appreciated in energy, power, petrochemical and other industries, which are the main fields where industrial security products are seen for the time being. Industrial magnates and traditional IT security giants seek to cover a wider range of industrial security solutions by acquisitions or business expansion, so as to dominate the industrial security market, and leverage their own influence to further expand market share and scope of business. Typical examples include Continental AG has acquired Argus, an Israel-based automotive cyber security company, to seek intelligent and safe driving services and solution; Harman International Industries has acquired TowerSec, a Michigan-based automotive cyber security company, to further guarantee the safety of its automotive products [23].

## 2.5   Application

In the advancement of the Industrial Internet, major developed countries have brought forward their own Industrial Internet strategies with different focuses in the light of respective actual national conditions. For example, the German Industry 4.0 strategy focuses on superimposing the new generation information technologies on existing industrial production devices to promote data integration and service sharing, and strengthen and upgrade hard manufacturing advantages with production and engineering technologies as its emphasis.

The U.S. Strategy for American Leadership in Advanced Manufacturing focuses on innovations in cutting-edge manufacturing technologies and the Industrial Internet, and stresses applying information technologies such as the Internet, big data and IoT to industries, thus transforming industrial production, products and services, promoting intelligent development of machinery equipment and changes in the business model, and maintaining intelligent data drive. Besides, both Germany and the U.S. have sped up the solicitation and promotion of pilot application programs to facilitate multi-industry coverage and multi-model construction, further expand their technological advantages.

**Germany focuses on industrial production to advance the application of the Industrial Internet.** Firstly, intelligent production of its *Plattform Industrie 4.0* gives impetus to the application of the Industrial Internet. Most projects have already completed verification through experiments and begin to be put into trial use and promoted, among which a few target production and management optimization. Secondly, automation and equipment enterprises lead the application of Industrial Internet projects. More than 12 industries have begun the application of the Industrial Internet, with the share of intelligent application by automation and equipment enterprises reaching 40%. Thirdly, the Industry 4.0 puts particular emphasis on integration of information and manufacturing technologies. The application of Industry 4.0 projects have popularized models such as quality management optimization, equipment failure prediction and production control integration. The well-known German manufacturer Siemens launched the MindSphere platform in 2016, based on which it provides the application of predictive maintenance, condition monitoring, energy data management and resource optimization. Currently, the MindSphere platform is used to monitor and test over 800,000 systems all over the world, including gas turbines, skyscrapers and traffic control centers. Siemens has developed a railway asset management scheme for the railway transportation industry, including functions applicable to all vehicles and infrastructure, such as remote monitoring, rapid diagnosis, failure prediction, which can be used to increase the availability and efficiency, reduce operational risks and costs, and improve the maintainability. Upon verification, the scheme has a Prescriptive maintenance validation availability of over 99%; delays have been reduced by 20% or more; GPS information has been applied to high-speed trains, enabling several hundred pieces of sensor data to be processed per second; and the time for complex troubleshooting has shortened by more than 20%. Bosch Group, as a global technology supplier, develops the IoT Suite and provides its customers with solutions and IoT applications.

Today, more than five million devices and machines have been widely interconnected via Bosch IoT Suite. Bosch has also tailored a solution for motor sports, which, by installing a wireless transmitter using 4G mobile technology in a car, can transmit data on the engine, location and speed to the receiver in the maintenance center, and enable almost real-time monitoring and analysis of car data based on Bosch IoT Suite.

**The U.S. is pushing forward the application of the Industrial Internet on a larger scale.** Firstly, a wide range of industries are covered, with a half being manufacturing. IIC application cases cover industries such as manufacturing, transport, retail, healthcare and agriculture, and manufacturing enterprises account for a half of all these enterprises. Secondly, manufacturing instances focus on intelligent production. Most of the manufacturing application projects use the mode of intelligent production, and only a few are customized. Thirdly, U.S. IT enterprises are integrated into manufacturing in virtue of their technological advantages to expand the scope of business. The U.S. software giant Microsoft has been promoting the Azure platform in recent years and established a partnership with Shanghai Zhenhua Heavy Industries Co., Ltd. (ZPMC), under which its offers Microsoft cloud manufacturing IoT platform to connect devices, analyze real-time data and gather data into the global monitoring center, thus helping ZPMC shift from a traditional manufacturer to a new generation digitalized intelligent port service provider. ZPMC is developing integrated machine learning and other advanced analysis services and building solutions such as predictive equipment maintenance, remote monitoring, service and operation system, so as to improve its efficiency and security as well as customer satisfaction. Based on the GE Predix platform, Exelon, a nuclear power company, has achieved higher energy harvesting through data acquisition by edge devices and a precise wind energy prediction model, creating value of USD two million every year.

# Chapter 3
# Development Status in China

## 3.1 Policy Deployment

**In China, the policy system for the Industrial Internet is gradually taking shape.** The CPC Central Committee and the State Council attach great importance to the development of the industrial internet. In November 2017, the State Council printed and released the *Guiding Opinions on Deepening the "Internet plus Advanced Manufacturing Industry" and Developing the Industrial Internet* (hereinafter referred to as the *Guiding Opinions*), a programmatic document guiding the development of the Industrial Internet in China. The *Guiding Opinions* puts forward "three-step" goals by 2025, 2035 and the mid-twenty-first century and proposes to establish three systems—network, platform and security systems, advance two applications, i.e., integrated innovation by large enterprises and application and popularization among SMEs, and build three pillars—industrial, ecological and international—and seven tasks. Since 2018, in order to further ensure that all work is carried out effectively, turn the strategy into plans and plans into actions, Ministry of Industry and Information Technology (MIIT) and other 22 ministries and commissions jointly developed the *Action Plan for the Development of the Industrial Internet (2018–2020)* in June 2018, to ensure the completion of the targets and tasks in the first stage, i.e., 2018–2020, set forth in the *Guiding Opinions*. Recently, guidance documents such as the *Implementation Plan for the Cultivation of Industrial Internet APPs (2018–2020)*, the *Guidelines for the Construction and Promotion of Industrial Internet Platforms*, the *Evaluation Methods of Industrial Internet Platforms* and the *Guiding Opinions on Strengthening Industrial Internet Security* have been or will be introduced in succession, and specific measures have been gradually detailed, indicating that China has basically established the policy system of "top-level programme + action plan + implementation guides" for the Industrial Internet [24–26].

**Relevant safeguard mechanisms for the Industrial Internet are gradually being established and perfected.** In order to put into practice the Guiding Opinions,

© China Science Publishing & Media Ltd (Science Press) 2020
Chinese Academy of Engineering, *Industrial Internet*,
https://doi.org/10.1007/978-981-15-7490-0_3

accelerate the development of the Industrial Internet and strengthen the overall planning and policy coordination for relevant work, in February 2018, the National Leading Group for the Upgrading the Country's Manufacturing Sector set up the Industrial Internet Working Group to make overall plans for and coordinate the development of the Industrial Internet, and the Industrial Internet Advisory Committee to provide strategic advice on the development of the Industrial Internet [27]. To promote the development of the Industrial Internet, MIIT, together with the Ministry of Finance, has launched the "Industrial Internet Innovative Development Program of 2018", which supported 91 projects and organized experiment and demonstration, with network, identification, platform, security and other key areas covered, guiding the innovative development of the Industrial Internet; advanced the construction of new industrialization demonstration bases for the Industrial Internet and supported Songjiang District, Shanghai in exploring the path of cluster-based Industrial Internet development. Efforts have also been made to apply the Industrial Internet to aviation, petrochemical, steel, home appliance, clothing, machinery and other industries and explore the way to establish several replicable empirical modes. Under the leadership of the Working Group, inter-ministerial cooperation and ministry-province coordination move forward steadily. The MIIT has concluded an agreement on strategic cooperation in the Industrial Internet with provinces and municipalities such as Shanghai and Zhejiang respectively to deepen its comprehensive cooperation with local governments in the light of the national key layout and local industrial characteristics, build model pilot projects and form empirical support that radiates its impacts across the country.

**Local governments have been vigorously promoting the implementation of Industrial Internet policies.** Local governments have actively put into practice the decisions and deployments made by the CPC Central Committee and the State Council, introduced local policies for the development of the Industrial Internet based on their respective realities to encourage, guide and support enterprises to build and apply the Industrial Internet, thus promoting normative and orderly development of the Industrial Internet. So far, more than 20 provinces, municipalities and autonomous regions, including Shanghai, Guangdong, Jiangsu and Zhejiang, have unveiled relevant policies, published implementation plans or action plans for the Industrial Internet and introduced related supporting measures, so as to make concerted efforts to accelerate the formation of an industrial ecosystem [1].

## 3.2   Network

**The top-level design for the network system has taken shape.** The network connection framework of the Industrial Internet is developed mainly by the Alliance of Industrial Internet (AII), which becomes the top-level design for building the network system. As is shown in Fig. 3.1, the network connection framework of the Industrial Internet has a two-level structure, namely internetworking and data communication; while internetworking is composed of two parts: factory internal

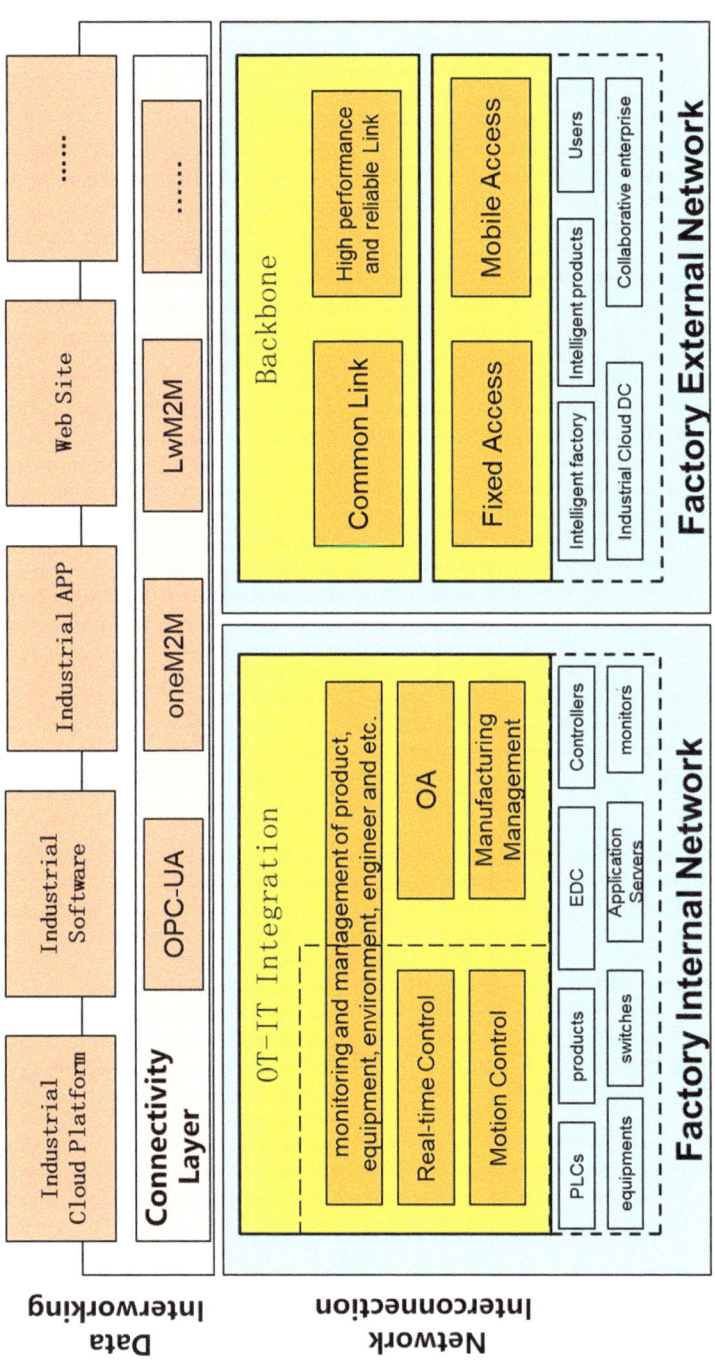

**Fig. 3.1** Network connection framework of the industrial internet

networks and factory external networks. The factory internal network is used to connect various elements within a factory, including personnel (e.g., production, design and external personnel), machines, (e.g., equipment and office facilities), materials (e.g., raw materials, WIP and finished products), environment (e.g., instrument and monitoring equipment), the corporate data center and application server, among others, which support business application within the factory. The factory external network is used to connect the smart factory, branches/partner enterprises, the industrial cloud data center, intelligent products, users and other subjects. With the factory external network, the data center/application server within the smart factory is interconnected with the industrial cloud data center outside the factory. The factory external network also enables the connection of branches/partner enterprises, users and intelligent products to the industrial cloud data center or corporate data center as configured. The data communication function in the Industrial Internet maintains seamless transmission of data and information between elements and between systems, so that heterogeneous systems can "understand" each other at the data level to achieve information integration and data interoperation [28, 29]. One of the key roles of the Industrial Internet is to eliminate information silos and guarantee cross-system data communication and integration. Therefore, the connection layer in data communication has to meet two requirements: one is to support the convergence of underlying data generated by various factory elements and products towards cloud platforms; the other is to provide multi-source heterogeneous data for upper-layer applications through factory internal networks and factory external networks, thus supporting diversified industrial applications.

**Preliminary progress has been made in the construction of network infrastructure for the Industrial Internet.** Firstly, operators have built external networks in different ways. China Unicom has built a physically isolated high-quality backbone network oriented towards manufacturing enterprises by upgrading and transforming the existing IP bearer network. China Telecom and China Mobile have explored ways to meet the high-quality network needs of the Industrial Internet through the SD-WAN technology based on the existing Internet. With wide coverage of mobile communication networks, all of the three operators had basically had their NB-IoT networks fully covering counties and cities all across the country by the end of 2018. Secondly, the transformation of IPv6 networks has been basically completed. By the end of 2018, these operators had completed IPv6 transformation of their 4G-LTE and fixed network equipment, preliminarily possessing the business support capacity. Thirdly, new network technologies have been gradually deployed, and innovative technologies such as industrial passive optical networks (PONs), IPv6 and edge computing have begun to be applied in enterprises from some industries [30]. Fourthly, the industry-university-research-application cooperation model has initially taken shape. Industries, universities, research institutes and enterprises have jointly built six network test beds in the AII, which cover key technologies such as TSN, 5G and SDN and have become important carriers of technology incubation, product R&D and application cultivation [31].

**The identifier resolution system has developed high capacity for independent innovation.** As is shown in Fig. 3.2, the technology system of the Industrial Internet

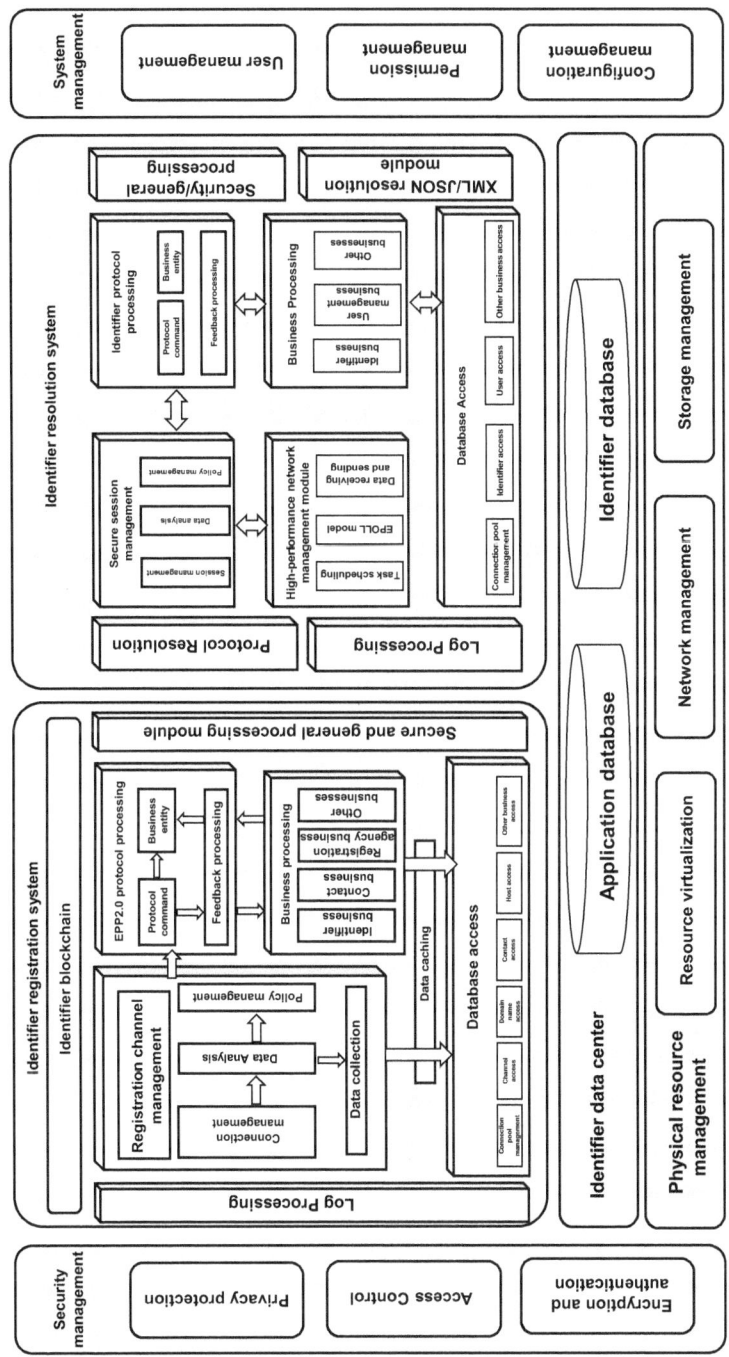

**Fig. 3.2** Architecture of industrial internet identifier resolution solutions

identifier resolution system incorporates identifier registration system, identifier resolution system, system management, security management and other necessary supporting systems. At present, participants in China's Industrial Internet identifier resolution system have preliminarily completed registration of identifiers with independent and proprietary intellectual property rights, authoritative resolution, recursive resolution and the R&D of the client software system technology, and established a core software system for the Industrial Internet identifier resolution system. China is carrying out the R&D of interconnection, identifier filing and emergency response systems, so as to gradually perfect its identifier resolution system. Research institutes in China have independently developed holistic solutions that comply with international standards such as DNS and Handle, gear themselves to more complex technical and application scenarios of the Industrial Internet and enable Industrial Internet identifier resolution to be compatible and unified. Such solutions, based on underlying hardware, provide high-performance registration and resolution systems, greatly improving performance indexes such as response time and throughput rate and effectively supporting upper-layer applications such as system management, privacy protection and encryption & authentication. They can be deployed to all links throughout the industrial chain of identifier resolution and really play the role of identity management in Industrial Internet applications.

**The Industrial Internet identifier resolution system is developing rapidly.** Firstly, the Industrial Internet has been systematically deployed. It has been launched and put into trial operation on five national top-tier nodes, such as Beijing, Shanghai, Guangzhou, Wuhan and Chongqing, and is being actively explored and constructed on a batch of second-level nodes, preliminarily forming four models of construction and operation on secondary-tier nodes, including vertical industrial services, third party services, public services and demonstration, thus laying a good foundation for further promoting the development and application of the Industrial Internet identifier resolution system secondary-tier nodes. Secondly, the application of identifier resolution has accelerated its innovative development and has been gradually launched in life cycle management of industrial goods, equipment asset management, supply chain management, product traceability and other links. For example, Shantui Janeoo Machinery Co., Ltd., a large state-owned backbone enterprise that has a long history in the production of concrete mixing and conveying machinery in China, has now begun to comprehensively apply the identifier resolution system to realize functions such as corporate product sales, management of after-sales services and tracking analysis of product contracts and archives. The identifier resolution system enables enterprises to transform their after-sales model from the traditional one to a paper-less and information-oriented one, bind product identification to contract information, and maintain modern repair and after-sales service processes, helps enterprises efficiently manage after-sales services and track the contract information of damaged equipment, ensures accurate and complete information as well as quick and convenient statistics. Through cooperation, enterprises only need to send information on failures and repairs via WeChat or other social tools rather than make repair calls, saving tedious work that management personnel copy and paste each piece of the contract information of damaged equipment for inquiry, increasing the working efficiency and improving the traditional after-sales services.

## 3.3   Platform

At present, with gradually improved integration of industrialization and IT development in China's manufacturing industry and increasingly diversified digital, network-based and intelligent products and services, the Industrial Internet enjoys a more and more solid foundation for platform construction and application in China.

**A variety of technologies and solutions oriented towards data acquisition are taking shape.** China's manufacturing is generally in the stage of transition from 2.0 to 3.0, with a relatively low proportion of digital and network-based production equipment, which was 44.8% in 2017 [32]. Challenged by difficult, expensive and inefficient data acquisition due to a large proportion of old equipment, low level of digitization and incompatible protocols, enterprises at home are actively exploring into a variety of technologies and solutions. On the one hand, Industrial Internet platforms such as CASICloud, ROOTCLOUD and HollySys have developed end-to-end data flow solutions for equipment and users through dummy equipment transformation, development of protocol conversion products and promotion of edge computing. On the other hand, China is witnessing the emergence of a number of SMEs that provide protocol compatibility and conversion solutions. Enterprises such as MJ Intelligent System, Inovance and Hualong Xunda have been actively developing intelligent gateways, intelligent controllers and other products that can make multiple protocols compatible and convertible, carrying out digital and network-based equipment transformation, so as to acquire data from main fieldbus, industrial Ethernet and Wireless Access Protocol (WAP) devices.

**China's common platform technology is mature, providing strong support for the construction of management platform in different industries.** China is on par with developed countries in terms of cloud computing and has a group of established cloud computing service providers such as Alibaba, Huawei and Tencent. Based on the mature and open Platform as a Service (PaaS), a number of operation technology (OT), information technology (IT) and communication technology (CT) enterprises in China have in succession begun to explore ways to build industry-oriented vertical management service platforms (industrial PaaS).

**Application software innovation is increasingly active, with a pattern where cloud migration of traditional software products and development of cloud industrial APPs move forward in a coordinated fashion.** Cloud migration is the basic trend in the current software industry and SaaS applications of Industrial Internet platforms come mainly from two sources. On the one hand, traditional R&D design tools, operation management software, manufacturing execution systems are undergoing cloud migration at a quicker pace. Enterprises such as Yonyou, Kingdee, Baosight and CAXA have been actively promoting the deployment for the development of software products based on cloud architectures and Yonyou has completed cloud migration of its financial and office software and CRM and other application software. On the other hand, the development and application of new industrial APPs are gradually rising. Some platform enterprises and start-ups have developed new industrial APPs based on cloud platforms for complex intelligent products such as engineering machinery, wind power, ships and high-speed rails and had these APPs commercialized. Following the new trend in the development of the Industrial Internet at present, leading enterprises in different industries in China are actively promoting strategic transformation of their businesses and expediting the construction of an industrial ecosystem based on Industrial Internet platforms.

**China's Industrial Internet platforms are entering a period of rapid development.** Firstly, the number of such platforms is growing fast. So far, over 50 platforms have cross-industry and cross-regional influence and some platforms have 100,000 pieces or sets of industrial equipment connected [33]. Secondly, these platforms have preliminarily established an industrial ecosystem and key software and hardware industries involving such platforms, such as industrial big data, industrial APP development, edge acquisition and intelligent gateway, have become development hotspots. An AII survey shows that among 168 platform technology suppliers, almost 80 have a size of more than 50 million RMB, accounting for nearly 50%. Thirdly, the number and engagement of developers focusing on ecosystem construction continue to increase. The number of users on the website of Huawei Developer Zone for the Industrial Internet has exceeded 10,000 and the First Industrial Big Data Innovation Competition organized by the China Academy of Information and Communications Technology (CAICT) attracted 1535 participants.

**China has preliminarily established an industrial development system for Industrial Internet platforms.** From the perspective of platform constructors, manufacturing enterprises, industrial equipment enterprises, industrial software enterprises and information & communication enterprises play a leading role in the construction of Industrial Internet platforms in China. For example, enterprises such as CASICloud, Sany, Haier, Shenyang Machine Tool, Yonyou and Huawei have pioneered in providing Industrial Internet platform services by virtue of their original capacity and market conditions, and expanded their businesses from the inside out. From the perspective of the application scope of platforms, Industrial Internet platforms are mainly applied in industries such as equipment, consumer products, electronic information and raw materials while application innovation based on Industrial Internet platforms is increasingly active in relevant fields, with a series of innovative applications such as quality improvement, process optimization, predictive equipment operation and maintenance, and supply chain collaboration formed and paying off. For example, ROOTCLOUD offers remote equipment operation & maintenance management solutions, maintaining access of 300,000 devices and real-time acquisition of over 5000 parameters; COSMO achieves fast empowerment through its mass customization model and is a gathering of 2.8 million design resources worldwide plus successful experience in interconnected factories; BIOP offers smelting process optimization and collaboration solutions, improving molten iron quality stability by 20%, saving 24 million RMB per year for each blast furnace and reducing 20,000 tons of carbon emissions [33].

**Chinese Industrial Internet platforms have some distinctive features in terms of application model.** Based on device connection and industrial data analysis capabilities, platforms at home have worked out a series of characteristic applications such as "platform + finance", "platform + insurance" and "platform + order", which carry out intelligent analysis through real-time production data generated by platform-connected devices, offer credit, insurance and other financial services that serve production and therefore help enterprises solve various practical problems in production. For example, Easylinking has created the "Shengyibang" platform, which provides order decomposition and subcontracting and production organization and management services, and has attracted 12,000 small and micro factories to conclude a partnership agreement and form a brand new business form of intelligent manufacturing crowdsourcing. Tengen Group facilitates the connection between customers and financial institutions based on real-time analysis of equipment operation data by its platform, to solve financing problems facing SMEs and lower the bad debt rate by more than 60%.

## 3.4 Security

**China's Industrial Internet has developed certain integrated defense capability.** Firstly, certain security control capability has been developed on the network side. Regulators concerned may, by collecting IP data flows regarding to Industrial Internet business and linking botnet, Trojan and worm detection systems and mobile Internet malicious program monitoring systems of basic telecom operators, obtain data on Industrial Internet assets, security events and threat intelligent upon analysis, and then deal with security events through operators' ability to block key nodes in backbone networks. Secondly, perceptions of networked key Industrial Internet devices have been improved. Currently, China has developed the ability to accurately identify high-risk vulnerabilities and risks in industrial control systems and industrial IoT devices exposed to the public network, whereby relevant regulators have completed security monitoring, inspection and rectification for the Industrial Internet. CAICT has actively promoted the construction of an Industrial Internet security monitoring platform featuring national, provincial and corporate three-level linkage, which, based on multi-dimensional data correlation and integration, builds the monitoring capacity combining active detection and passive flow analysis, and has a ministerial-provincial-corporate three-level architecture. The monitoring radiates from the platform to Industrial Internet assets such as networked devices and industrial APPs. So far, it has covered hundreds of key Industrial Internet platforms, totally more than 40 types of approximately two million devices, and such industries as manufacturing, transportation, information transmission and technology services. Thirdly, the security protection capability of the Industrial Internet has constantly been improved. The new generation industrial firewalls and intrusion detection products independently developed by China have gradually become mature and widely applied in Industrial Internet enterprises [34].

**The industry-university-research-application coordinated development platform has been gradually established.** The AII has specially set up a security group, which, since its establishment, has achieved a number of results in standards development, testing & validation, industrial promotion and international cooperation. In September 2018, the AII released the Industrial Internet Security Framework, which, built from three perspectives, namely the object of protection, protection measures and protection management, aims at guiding Industrial Internet enterprises to deploy security protection measures and increase their security protection capacity. Additionally, the AII has also released a number of reports on Industrial Internet security, for example, the Reference Scheme on Industrial Cloud Security Protection, A Collection of Cases of Typical Industrial Internet Security Solutions (Release 1.0) and the Report on the Industrial Internet and Security Situation (Annual Report. Industries have in succession made arrangements to improve Industrial Internet security and traditional security vendors have increased their investments in Industrial Internet security and offered Industrial Internet enterprises with security technologies, products and solutions by making use of their existing advantages. Meanwhile, a number of enterprises that concentrate on Industrial Internet security research have gradually emerged and kept a foothold in industries, injecting new impetus into the development of Industrial Internet security. In order to normalize the assessment and evaluation of Industrial Internet security, establish an Industrial Internet security assessment and evaluation system, and cultivate personnel engaged in such assessment and evaluation, a pilot program for training of Industrial Internet security appraisers has been launched within the AII. The MIIT has carried out the selection of pilot and model cyber security projects and selected outstanding Industrial Internet security projects, thus promoting the popularization and application of security technologies. At the same time, it has selected representative areas featuring good industrial development to support the construction of Industrial Internet security demonstration areas. Moreover, the MIIT has actively organized the application for support from the Industrial Internet Innovative Development Program (for Security) of 2018, in which the security involves mainly the construction of an Industrial Internet security system, the construction of a favorable environment for Industrial Internet security assessment tests and experimental verification, and capacity building, promotion and application of common services for Industrial Internet security.

## 3.5   Application

China keeps up with the rest of the world in terms of Industrial Internet application and has developed some characteristic application models.

**The platform-based optimization of equipment assets has become a hotpot of application.** In this process, Internet access and performance optimization of devices are the key. For example, oriented towards key industries such as engineering machinery and auto & parts, Changsha Industrial Cloud Platform offers platform-based predictive equipment maintenance services. Information like remote operating condition and status of equipment gathers in the platform through the multi-protocol bus data integration technology, which information will undergo preprocessing, feature extraction and anomaly detection, and then the failure prediction algorithm model and real-time data flows will be combined to achieve real-time analysis, judgment and failure prediction in respect of equipment operation. At present, the platform has connected more than 143,000 pieces of industrial equipment and has 2000 TB of industrial data in stock. Statistics of enterprises to which the platform has offered services indicate that the platform has reduced the time for after-sales repairs by 30%, lower maintenance costs by 30%, increase customer satisfaction by more than 30%, raise the product pass rate by 10% and improve the average productivity by approximately 16% for industrial enterprises. Another example is IAP Technology, a subsidiary of Histron Technology, which integrates most of the mainstream communication protocols in the market by developing an Industrial Automatic Platform (IAP) edge router, and then collects data on industrial equipment in a real-time manner; it employs visual and dynamically monitored communication configurations to facilitate connection and integration of equipment. This solution is applied in a number of power plants under Fujian Energy Group, such as Hongshan Thermal Power Plant and Jinjiang Gas Power Plant, enabling the Group to increase its production and operation profit by 8% and lowering its production cost by 20%; it is also applied in Shenzhen Beyond Sci-tech Co., Ltd., helping the enterprise realize real-time collection of all production data and remote monitoring of production equipment, thus increasing the labor productivity by 8–10% and greatly reducing equipment downtime [35].

**Application scenarios where the production process is optimized with the aid of the Industrial Internet continue to be deepened.** For example, BEACON, the Industrial Internet platform owned by Foxconn, supports 28 communication protocols through the CorePro module and allows the access of 16 types of equipment; it is now connecting and managing nearly 700,000 pieces of industrial equipment, with the total number of equipment data collection points exceeding seven million. Through analysis and utilization of mass equipment data and production process data, the output per capita of the electronic components surface mounting workshop has grown by 20% and the manufacturing yields have increased by more than 30%; Meanwhile, the optimization of the supply chain system based on the platform, which visualizes order delivery, has shortened the enterprise's inventory cycle by 15% and raised the overall efficiency by up to 30%. For another example, Hualong Xunda and Qujing Cigarette Factory of Hongyunhonghe Group have jointly explored the digital twin manufacturing model for tobacco production, which, based on Tencent Jupiter Cloud, an Industrial Internet platform, and by building mappings and interactions between physical workshops, such as tobacco processing, wrapping, modeling and logistics, and virtual workshops, enables connection and integration of all elements, processes and business data, and forms virtual manufacturing services for the tobacco industry. In the process of trial operation, the roll-packing productivity increased by 3.12%, the efficiency of equipment on the moulding line rose by 1.8% and the training cycle of workers on the production line was shortened from 180 days to 45 days [36, 37].

**Highlights are observed in the provision of application services featuring industry-finance integration for SMEs through platforms.** For example, Tengen has built an industrial credit cross-validation model by converging and analyzing the data on sold production equipment through the I-Martrix Industrial Internet platform, thus providing more than 13,000 medium-sized, small and micro enterprises with big data credit services and allowing them to obtain over 800 million RMB of loans a year. For another example, Tangshan Chenglian E-Business project, by maintaining unobstructed port connections with supply chain management platforms downstream and in relevant industries, and through active cooperation with financial institutions, has gradually refined the granularity of the good faith index of trading enterprises and developed risk control models of different types and with different focuses in the light of the characteristics of upstream, midstream and downstream enterprises, thus perfecting the platform's good faith index credit system. Currently, the platform has been applied in China CITIC Bank, where the number of transactions has exceeded 10,000, the amount of online transactions has reached more than one billion RMB and the number of users has reached over 6000, supporting medium-sized, small and micro enterprises in increasing trading efficiency and capital turnover and reducing supply chain operating costs [38].

**The application of the Industrial Internet in vertical fields is speeding up its pace.** More and more enterprises have realized that the implementation path of the Industrial Internet should take into full account the characteristics of different industries and ensure effective understanding, conversion and output of relevant mechanisms in industries [39, 40]. ZTT Group, for example, focuses on understanding mechanism models and algorithms in the cable industry and promoting the output of these mechanism models. Firstly, ZTT provides basic information-oriented management suites for SMEs to ensure low-cost and rapid deployment for IT development; secondly, it provides high-level big data analysis, early warning and forecast for large enterprises by using the industry-specific mechanism algorithms and models offered by the platform, thus helping cable enterprises better optimize their operation and management decisions [41]; thirdly, it provides industrial e-commerce, supply chain financing, production capacity sharing and other services in order for model innovation. At present, it has sorted out ways to deal with protocols and basic data concerning more than 200 types of production and testing equipment in the cable industry and completed the construction of more than 100 cable-related models and algorithms. Based on this, it can enable cable equipment to work on the cloud in 10 min and, through specific models and algorithms in the cable industry, rapidly realize the application of industrial APPs such as automatic optical fiber distribution and analysis of fiber cut rates [42].

## 3.6 Standardization

Standards have always been a key factor determining the leadership in an industry and of vital importance to the technical development route, industrial system design and industrialization of an emerging industry. China attaches great importance to the standardization of the Industrial Internet [43–45].

The AII has set up a working group on technology and standard research, which takes charge of the development of standards in the light of the requirements of Industrial Internet standardization. In February 2017, the AII released the Framework of Industrial Internet Standard System (Release 1.0), which states the general idea, basic principles, framework, key directions of standardization and suggestions on standardization promotion for the construction of the Industrial Internet Standard System, providing reference and basis for the formulation of national, industrial and organizational Industrial Internet standards. As at the end of November 2018, the AII had developed and released eight alliance standards whilst having three under research and nine approved, which covered basic standards for network, platform, security and other aspects [46, 47].

In September 2017, with the guidance from the MIIT, China Communications Standards Association (CCSA) set up the Special Taskforce on the Industrial Internet (ST8) to allow full play to the industrial cluster advantage of standardization organizations and arouse the enthusiasm of all stakeholders of standardization, so as to make concerted efforts to push for sound progress in the normative and scale development of the Industrial Internet and seek a greater say in the international Industrial Internet standardization [48]. By the end of November 2018, two national standards, namely the *Industrial Internet: Overall Network Architecture* and the *Intelligent Manufacturing: Requirements of the Identifier Resolution System*, and 25 industrial standards had been approved, and eight other industrial standards had been submitted for approval.

At the end of 2017, the *Guiding Opinions* stressed in the Basic Situation part that an unsound standard system is one of the key factors influencing the development of the Industrial Internet in China. It contains important deployment for the standardization of the Industrial Internet: firstly, the working mechanism for the standardization of the Industrial Internet should be perfected, for which it proposes to "set up a national coordination group, general working group and advisory group for the standardization of the Industrial Internet to make overall planning for the construction of a standard system for the Industrial Internet, optimize relevant mechanisms and accelerate the construction of a unified and open standard system for the Industrial Internet." Secondly, R&D of standards should be accelerated, thus it proposes to "formulate an overall standard and a number of basic common standards, application standards and security standards." Thirdly, testing and validation of standards should be carried out, for which it proposes to "organize the R&D, testing and demonstration of standards, and simultaneously advance the testing and validation of the content of standards, the construction of a favorable environment for such testing and validation as well as the development and promotion of simulating and testing tools." Fourthly, multilateral dialogues and cooperation should be strengthened, for which it proposes to "strengthen collaboration with international organizations, jointly formulate standards, norms and international rules on the Industrial Internet and establish a multilateral, democratic and transparent international governance system for the Industrial Internet" [24].

In order to implement the working requirements set forth in the *Guiding Opinions*, the MIIT has been actively promoting relevant standardization work. In early 2018, the MIIT launched the preparation of the working mechanism scheme for standardization and the guidelines for comprehensive standardization of the Industrial Internet, promoted the R&D of organizational standards by CCSA and organized Industrial Internet standardization testing and demonstration projects. Also, it cooperated with Industrial Internet/intelligent manufacturing standardization organizations from the U.S., Germany and other countries to jointly carry forward the standardization of the Industrial Internet [49].

# Chapter 4
# Innovative Development

## 4.1 Architecture 2.0

The Industrial Internet Architecture (Version 1.0) was officially released in September 2016, provided a clear and simplifed methodology for the industries and have been reached a broad consensus on the development of the Industrial Internet. After 2 years of exploration and practice, the industries have accumulated more extensive experiences, in addition with the emergence of various new technologies which drives the architecture upgradation toward more systematic and prospective [50], such as edge computing, AI and etc. According with large amount of research on the existing typical architectures patterns and core standards abroad, the Industrial Internet Architecture V2.0 is built in the light of a comprehensive methodology as the, which contains three types of views on business, function and implementation. It reflect the value concept of "demand oriented, capacity leaded, function defined and implementation guided", with the structured presentation of "data flow-oriented, top-down, layered mapping and stepwise refinement", and construct with the principle on "integration of industrial, software and communication methodologies, and embodies with the three elements of network, data and security".

In general, the business view summarized the business demand and key processes on the application side, specified the value of the Industrial Internet and exported five key capabilities, which use to identify the application combinability of scenarios and models. The essence is to solve the value would bring for the Industrial Internet and capabilities should be required for the enterprises to process. The function view has established the core function modules and their interaction relationships, defined the scope of core functions and summarized the relationship between the element of network, data and security with new technologies support. The nature is to finalize the functions used to support the business implementation above. Furthermore, the implementation view defined the subject, layer and scope of system implementation; simplified the key technologies, systems, software and hardware modules and their

© China Science Publishing & Media Ltd (Science Press) 2020
Chinese Academy of Engineering, *Industrial Internet*,
https://doi.org/10.1007/978-981-15-7490-0_4

interrelations; and affirmed the information flows for the implementation scenarios, such as data flows and control flows. The nature is solving the issue in the actual application deployment to complete the above functions.

Specifically, the business view reflects the vision, objective and value of the Industrial Internet, come up with the five core capabilities to provide guidance and reference in respect of personnel functions, business processes and business strategies, etc. Under the business level, it helps the CEO and middle management of a company to establish the vision, objectives and direction of optimization, and the two fundamental objectives are reducing costs and promoting value of the company, which can be achieved through specific scheme such as increasing efficiency, improving services and quality, and developing new business models. In order to implement these business concerns in the context of digital transformation, the enterprises are required to have five key capabilities, which includes all the factors on ubiquitous perception, such as personnel, equipment, materials, regulations and environment, etc.; agile response customer demand and market change; flexible allocation and coordination of the global resources; dynamical optimization of the productive activities; and intelligence decisions. The demand for these capabilities varies with application scenarios and the subsequent function view also contains mapping relationship with the five capabilities.

As shown in Fig. 4.1, based on the concepts of value guidance and layered mapping, the updated business view in the Industrial Internet Architecture V2.0 provides more guidance for the industrial enterprises with improved implementation operability.

As shown in Fig. 4.2, take manufacturing as example, enterprises have different emphasis of required capabilities in the various application scenarios, such as collaborative design and flexible reconstruction of a production line, thus enterprises have to varies the required capabilities during the plan and deploy of relevant functions.

As shown in Fig. 4.3, the function view focuses on how to build core capabilities through the Industrial Internet, describe and define various key function modules

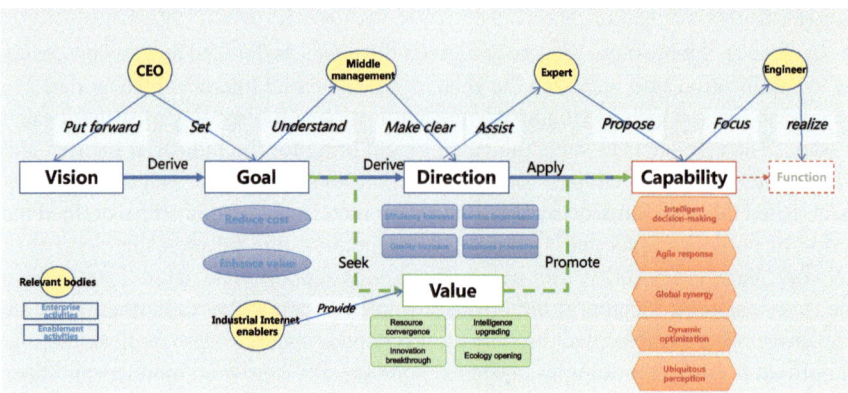

**Fig. 4.1** Business view of the industrial internet architecture V2.0

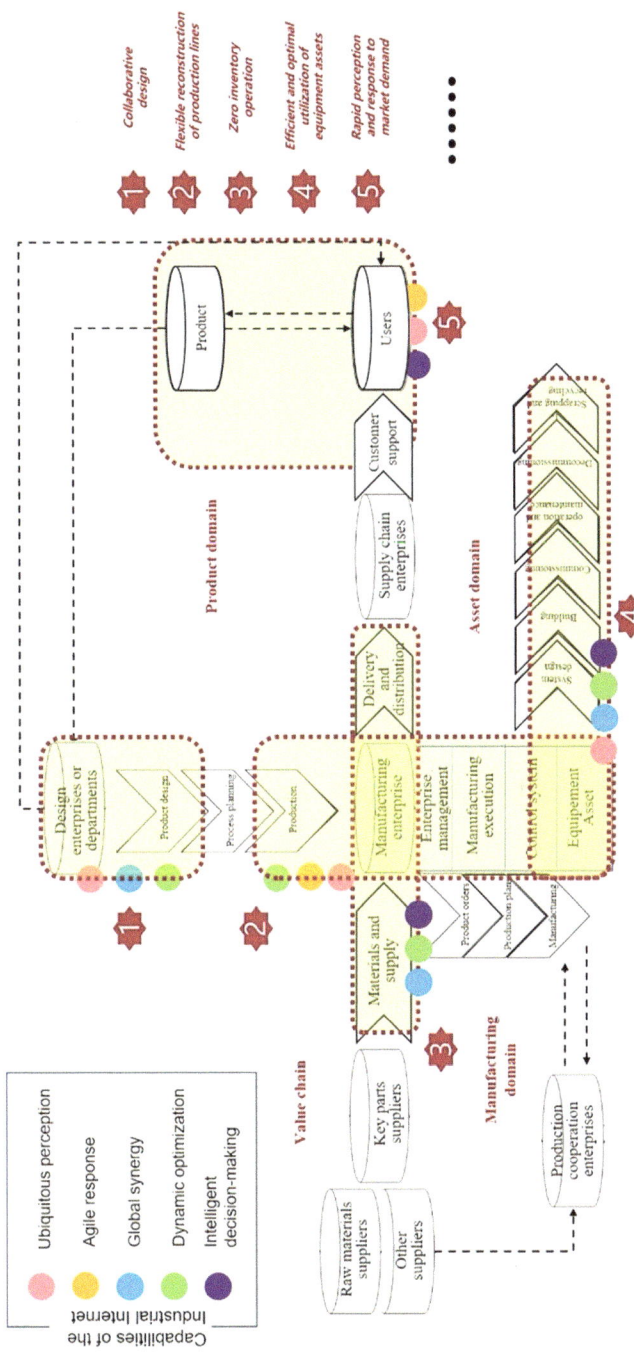

**Fig. 4.2**  Example of applying the business view to manufacturing

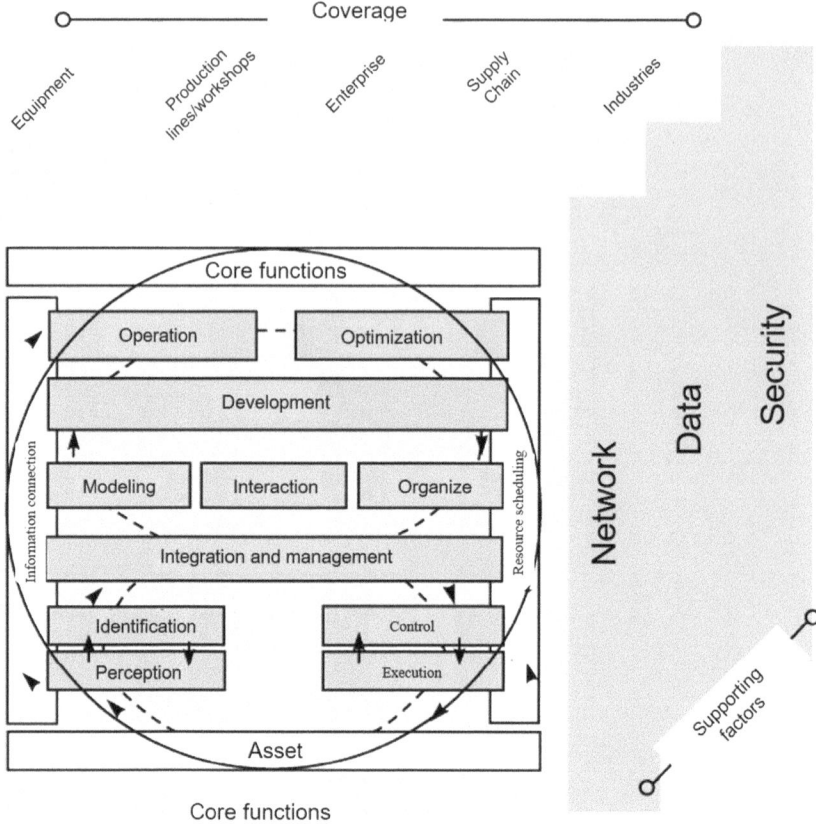

**Fig. 4.3** Function view of the industrial internet architecture V2.0

between lower-level assets to upper-layer business implementation and their internal logical relations, including two types of space, three layers and three closed loops. The two types of space refer to the physical space of underlying assets perception and execution from the CPS perspective, and the upper-layer information space of control, modeling, interaction, optimization and others. Furthermore, the three layers include the connection layer, management layer and application layer. For the connection layer, it is providing with functions of perception, identification, control and execution, which focuses on data acquisition and real-time control; For the management layer, it is providing with functions of integration and management, modeling, interaction and organization, which focuses on virtual data mapping and management organization; For the application layer, it is providing with functions of development, operation and optimization, which focuses on data mining analysis and value conversion. Moreover, he three closed loops include those of control, optimization and value. The closed loop of control represents the real-time operation capability between the connection layer and the management layer; the closed loop of optimization represents the optimization capability orientation between the management layer and the application layer; at last, the closed loop of value represents the capability of value innovation that drives improvements in business capability based on complete Industrial Internet functions.

As shown in Fig. 4.4, the implementation view based on the layered thinking, guiding the enterprises to make actual deployments for the application of the Industrial Internet on equipment, edge, intra-enterprise and cross-enterprise layers [51].

The equipment layer consists of industrial equipment and industrial products. Overall, the complex bottom layer of industrial equipment and products is provided with functions such as sensing and execution, above which there are functions such as data, model and application. Indeed, the simple industrial products have the perception function only.

On the edge layer lie edge computing nodes, industrial computers or industrial intelligent terminals. Edge computing nodes are the carrier of "sinking" cloud-based functions, with typical functions such as equipment management, data analysis and service application hosting. Industrial computers or industrial intelligent terminals are typical man-machine interaction devices [52, 53].

The intra-enterprise layer means the enterprise platform that hosts main functions of the Industrial Internet, from the connection management to equipment model management towards the basic data management and analysis as well as complete application service management.

The cross-enterprise layer means any industrial platforms that converges a number of enterprise platforms, guarantees end-to-end data transmission through SDN and maintains interconnection among multiple platform models through asset management whilst carrying out management of the status and functions of mass devices, systematic management of IT resources, reasonable arrangement and allocation of complex industrial events. This layer is provided with a relatively comprehensive environment supporting application development.

## 4.2   Time-Sensitive Network

Time-Sensitive Network (TSN) is a new-type network technology oriented towards industrial intelligent production, which provides the industrial production environment with a type of network that supports high-rate and high-bandwidth data acquisition and guarantees highly-real-time control information transmission.

In the traditional industrial production environment, a large number of industrial applications (e.g., machine control, process control, robot control, etc.) have an urgent demand for real-time communication to ensure efficient and safe completion of all production processes. In present, the common practice to meet this requirement is to modify the Ethernet protocol of an enterprise internal network or deploy an independent dedicated Ethernet network in the key production process. However, perusing to the issue of inadequate connectivity, extensibility, and compatibility of

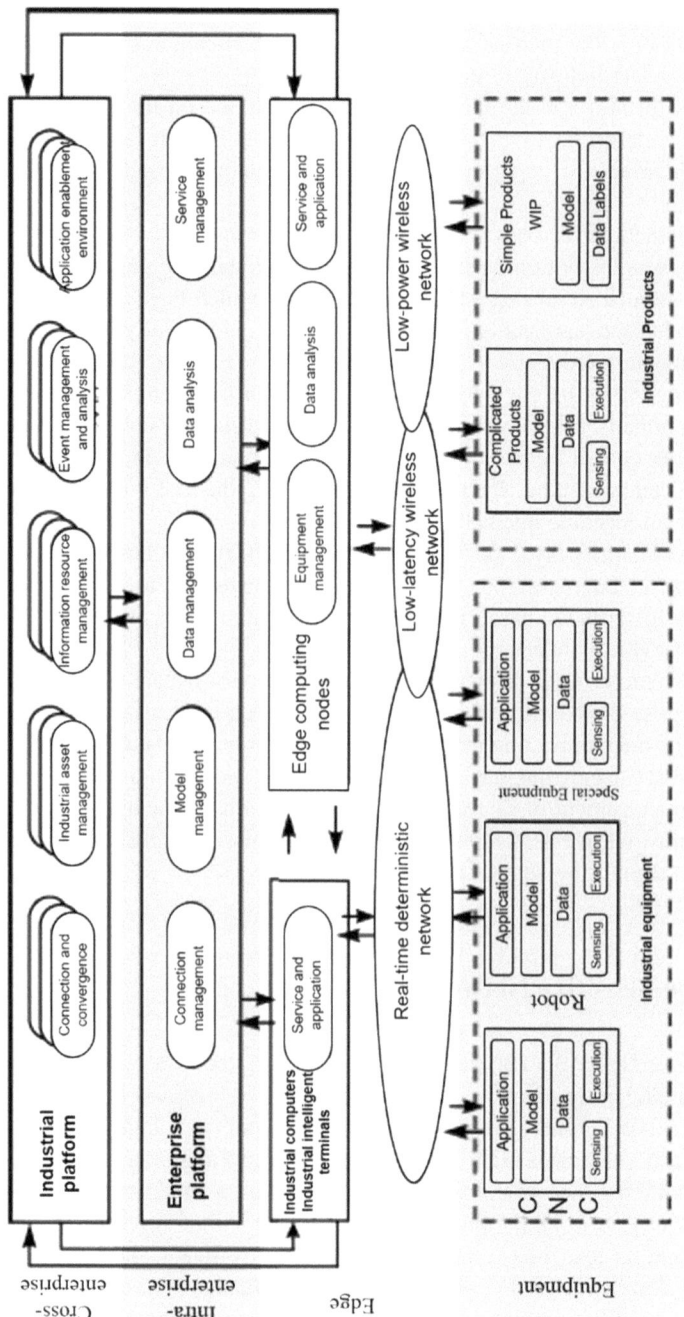

**Fig. 4.4** Implementation view of the industrial internet architecture V2.0

the practice, and it is increasingly apparent in the process of the upgrade from the traditional plant control network (PCN) to the Industrial Internet. Therefore, the TSN offers an effective solution to this issue.

TSN is a high-quality real-time transmission network with bounded transmission latency, low transmission jitter and extremely low data loss rate. Based on the standard Ethernet, it ensures real-time, efficient, stable and secure transmission of time-sensitive data through a number of optimization mechanisms such as time synchronization, data scheduling and load shaping. In short, TSN maintains deterministic real-time communication in the network through a global clock and a transmission scheduler connecting network components. The scheduler controls the actual transmission time and path of time-sensitive data flows according to the corresponding scheduling policy, so as to avoid transmission performance reduction and unpredictability caused by the competition for links and then to ensure point-to-point real time communication of time-sensitive applications.

For now, IEEE 802.1 is pushing the formulation of TSN series standards, mainly covering time synchronization, data frame control, data flow scheduling, transmission reliability guarantee and other protocols. China is also promoting the development of TSN series standards for the Industrial Internet.

The TSN technology makes it possible to change the status of "an absence of universal standards" for communication within industrial networks and in the future, and manufacturers will be able to carry out data protocol design and application development based on the unified basic network "TSN + IPv6", changing the current "stovepipe-type" industrial pattern. Towards the 1000 Mbit/s interface design, TSN is compatible with the widely use of 100 M interfaces in industrial networks and therefore is a promising technology solution that evolves to gigabit Ethernet. Industrial Ethernet networks such as PROFINET, EtherCAT and SERCOS III are probing into the compatibility, interconnectivity and evolution with the TSN technology.

TSN, as a data link layer (DLL) technology, with excellent capability to support for the upper layers' compatibility. Firstly, TSN has changed the "stovepipe model" of the traditional industrial Ethernet technology, which brings better support for different protocols such as IP/IPv6 and TCP/UDP to facilitate the integration of OT and IT network layered structures; Secondly, TSN will build a perfect YANG data model, which is well compatible with YANG data models of upper-layer technologies such as DetNet and SDN, so as to better support various upper-layer applications; thirdly, the collaboration between TSN and OPC-UA can solve factory internal data communication problems, extend OPC-UA data acquisition to the work cell and thus achieve collection of all-round real-time data on the production environment.

The transmission latency of time-sensitive data flows is absolutely guaranteed, and has a certain upper bound. In the traditional network, latency is usually guaranteed through bandwidth allocation, which makes the network uncertain and unpredictable; in opposite, TSN can eliminate such uncertainty and unpredictability, and enable the allocated bandwidth to satisfy the required latency and then allow bandwidth allocation to meet actual application requirements, not only increasing the bandwidth utilization ratio, but also guaranteeing transmission latency upper bounds.

TSN supports hybrid transmission of time-sensitive and non-time-sensitive data flows in the same network without the risk of mutual interference. In a traditional network, data flows are transmitted in the "Best-effort" service model. When two types of data flows mixed together, the scheduling and transmission of non-time-sensitive data flows will influence that of time-sensitive data flows, so that the transmission latency of time-sensitive data flows cannot be guaranteed. On the contrary, in the TSN the scheduler gives top priority to time-sensitive data and ensures stable and real-time transmission of time-sensitive data flows through preemption mechanism, traffic shaping mechanism or otherwise, eliminating mutual interference between data flows.

TSN provides stable data transmission as network switching devices smoothly forward data flows through the traffic shaping mechanism. In the traditional network, it is inevitable for the sudden of peak load. Such unsteady flows disable effective prediction of transmission latency in data forwarding, making it hard to guarantee real-time data transmission. In the TSN, a switching device shapes the received load, especially carrying out peak traffic caching and tries to forward it smoothly. This mechanism guarantees stable and predictable data transmission and ensures end-to-end transmission latency of time-sensitive data.

## 4.3  5G and Industrial Wireless Communication

Globally, the industrial automation research institutes and ICT enterprises are engaging in the research and standardization of industrial wireless communication, which mainly include operator-led cellular mobile communication technologies, such as NB-IoT, 4G and 5G, and unlicensed wireless network technologies such as WIA-PA/FA and MulteFire.

The 5G Ultra Reliable & Low Latency Communication (uRLLC) is a 5G optimization technology for the Industrial Internet, which meets industrial control application requirements in industrial highly-reliable and low-latency scenarios. In early 2016, the 3GPP, an international mobile communication standard organization, launched the formulation of standards for 5G technologies, and completed the development of R15 standards for uRLLC Phase I in June 2018, indeed, the 3GPP is planning to complete the standardization of uRLLC in 3GPP R16 by September 2019 [54, 55].

Compared with previous 4G and other cellular wireless communication technologies, 5G uRLLC has introduced a number of low-latency and highly reliable key technologies, which will greatly increase the system performance [56]. In terms of low latency, main 5G uRLLC technologies include: introducing smaller time resource units, such as mini-slot, adopting a scheduling license-free mechanism for uplink access, allowing direct access of terminals to the channel, supporting asynchronous processes to save uplink synchronization costs and employing rapid

Hybrid Automatic Repeat Request (HARQ) and rapid dynamic scheduling, among others. In terms of reliability, the 5G uRLLC technologies mainly include: adopting retransmission mechanisms, more robust multi-antenna transmission diversity mechanisms, highly robust coding and modulation orders (MCS selection) and super robust channel state estimation. Meanwhile, 5G uRLLC also supports IEEE 1588v2-based synchronization technologies. In a motion control scenario, 5G uRLLC can maintain sub-microsecond highly precise time synchronization through wireless interface in a communication group of 50–100 devices. The current reliability index of 5G uRLLC is: the user-plane latency of uplink and downlink IP data packet/message transmission between the base station and a terminal is less than 1 ms and the reliability of transmitting 32-byte packets at a time is 99.999%; when 5G standards are finally developed, the index is expected to be further enhanced.

NB-IoT is a cellular-based emerging technology for cellular data connection of low-power devices in a wide area network (WAN), which can meet data acquisition needs of the Industrial Internet [57]. 3GPP completed the development of NB-IoT R13 standards in June 2016 and R14 standards in August 2017.

NB-IoT has a distinct advantage in the Industrial Internet application. It has a wider coverage, provides a 20 dB gain in the coverage of existing LTE networks through technologies such as high transmit power spectrum diversity in the same frequency band, control channel and data retransmission, and antenna diversity, which also satisfy the needs of factories, underground tube wells and other applications that require deep coverage in the Industrial Internet; NB-IoT provides more than 50–100 times connections than the existing wireless technologies through technologies such as congestion and overload control and smaller scheduling granularity, a single sector is able to support 100,000 connections, it required to satisfy the demand for large-scale data acquisition in factories; NB-IoT complete with low power consumption through technologies such as Power Saving Mode (PSM) and extended Discontinuous Reception (eDRX), and enabling battery-powered devices to work for years, also satisfy the remote monitoring needs of Industrial Internet with distanced environmental equipment.

MulteFire is a wireless technology developed by MulteFire Alliance to operate in unauthorized spectrum (such as the global 5 GHz, 2.4 G and Sub-1 G). It aims to combine the performance advantages of LTE and the Wi-Fi-like simplicity, so as to provide better network coverage than Wi-Fi (less dead zones) with more secure authentication mechanism and better network performance, thus ensuring better user experience and satisfying various Industrial Internet control and data acquisition needs. In January 2017, MulteFire Alliance completed the specification MulteFire Release 1.0 and the MulteFire Release 1.1 released at the end of 2017 add on the characteristics of coverage enhancement and NB-IoT [58].

At present, the MulteFire wireless network technology includes both broadband and narrowband solutions: LTE-U for broadband and IoT-U for narrowband. The MulteFire LTE-U uses up to 80 MHz bandwidth, provides a coverage distance more than 2–3 times that of Wi-Fi, and more a single cell can support more than 50 concurrent terminals, two-way authentication between terminals and base stations, AES 128/256-bit air interface data encryption, ensures security between base stations and application platforms through IPsec, and is provided with the perfect Grade 9 communication QoS guarantee mechanism. Based on 3GPP's revision to the NB-IoT technology and in the light of regulations on unlicensed spectrum, the MulteFire IoT-U boasts advantages such as wide coverage (the coverage radius can reach 0.5–1 km), low power consumption (if a terminal reports once daily, 200 bytes at a time, then a 2400 mAh battery can support 10 years of standby) and large connections (each station supports the access of 5000 devices) in addition to the same security as the MulteFire LTE-U.

WIA-PA, as a wireless standard for industrial process automation, subjects its physical and MAC layers to IEEE 802.15.4-related standards and has autonomously defined network and application layers, which are mainly used for information collection, process measurements and other relevant services in industrial processes. WIA-PA guarantees real-time, reliable and flexible industrial data transmission through the 802.15.4 super frame structure, which uses a hybrid access model of Carrier Sense Multiple Access (CSMA) and Time Division Multiple Access (TDMA); effectively restrains sudden interference through the multi-channel adaptive frequency modulation mechanism and safeguards the transmission of industrial data in the complicated electromagnetic environment in factories; and guarantees reliable end-to-end industrial data transmission through highly reliable new-type wireless local area network (WLAN) routing [59].

Wireless Network for Industrial Automation—Factory Automation (WIA-FA) is a wireless data transmission technology tailored to the requirements of factory automation such as high real time and high reliability. In 2014, WIA-FA was released as a publicly available specification of the International Electrotechnical Commission (IEC). WIA-FA guarantees the reliability of industrial data transmission by such means as data priority-based scheduling and repeated retransmission; and ensure the industrial data transmission latency through a combined allocation of preemption and fixed assignment.

## 4.4   Edge Computing

In the global trends of industrial digital transformation, various of traditional services are undergoing changes such as communication, traveling, education and healthcare. In order to meet the demand of the Industrial Internet for agile connections, real-time services, data optimization, application intelligence, security and privacy protection in this transformation process, the edge computing offers intelligent services on the edge of networks and enables an integration of network, computing, storage and application capabilities through distributed open systems [60, 61]. With continuous evolution of the Industrial Internet edge computing technology and accelerated upgradation of industries, which required a clear cognition and overall arrangements for the edge computing development.

As a distributed computing architecture, the edge computing improves the performance of network services, opens edge data and stimulates new models and business formats on the edge of networks with converging network, computing, storage, application and intelligence as the five type of resources [62]. The edge computing of the Industrial Internet is a one of the focus of those engaged in the Industrial Internet locally and abroad, as it not only solves practical problems in industrial production, but also enables new impetus into the transformation of industries.

The edge computing of the Industrial Internet can solve the complex problems caused by a large number of heterogeneous devices and networks on industrial sites. Industries should produce a variety of products in the light of market demand while the development of industrial productivity is a process of accumulation and gradual upgrading, which makes the industrial environment is complicated and diversified. For instance, there are more than 30 different communication protocols on traditional industrial sites. And the connections between industrial equipment require "field-level" computing power of edge computing to facilitate conversion and interconnection between different kinds of network communication protocols, whilst addressing great challenges from heterogeneous network deployment and configuration, network management and maintenance.

The edge computing of the Industrial Internet has to ensure to solve the issue of real-time and reliability in industrial production. In some industrial control scenarios, the computing latency should be controlled within 10 ms. If both data analysis and control logic are implemented on the cloud, it is difficult to meet the real time requirement. Meanwhile, in industrial production, computing is required to be able to "survive locally" regardless of network transmission bandwidth and load, so as to avoid impacts of accidental factors such as Internet shutdown and excessive latency on real-time production. Edge computing can meet the requirements of the Industrial Internet for real-time and reliable services.

The edge computing should have the capability of "opening devices and sharing data" required by the transformation and upgrade of industries. At present, most of the industrial production equipment and devices in factories are "dummy ones". On one side, these devices usually use in the closed systems featuring hardware and software integration, disabling sharing of the production process data collected; on the other hand, the diversity of equipment manufacturers leads to inconsistent standards for equipment/device data and failure of mutual recognition, thus impeding a greater role of data. In fact, intelligent production, network-based collaboration, personalized customization and service-oriented extension required by the Industrial Internet all demand a change brought about by edge computing to "dummy devices" on industrial sites to achieve data opening and unification [63].

The Industrial intelligence requires a new model of "edge-cloud coordination". There exists massive and complete real-time data on edge nodes in the Industrial Internet. For example, based on AT&T estimates that self-driving cars can generate 3.6 TB of data per hour, the U.S. has deployed more than 30 million surveillance cameras, which generate over four billion hours of massive video data every week [63]. The edge is considered as a place of complete and latest data. Edge computing can complement cloud platforms in analysis and application of industrial data and the development of industrial intelligence to form a new model of "edge-cloud coordination", so as to combine AI and other new technologies with cloud and edge platforms respectively, bring a new driving force for business process optimization, operation & maintenance automation and business innovation with respect to the Industrial Internet and then bring about significant efficiency improvement and cost advantage.

In 2015, the edge computing entered an era of rapid growth, during which it aroused close attention of academic and industrial circles at home and abroad given its ability to meet the demand for Internet of everything [64].

The edge computing drives the Industrial Internet into two clearly technical paths. One is to provide Industrial Internet applications with computing power through the "sinking" of ICT infrastructure, for example, completing the deployment for edge cloud. The edge cloud technology turns traditional centralized data centers into small data centers that are deployed on the edge of networks to provide industrial users with computing power on demand. At the end of 2017, enterprises like China Unicom, Intel and Tencent jointly built a test bed for edge data centers and they plan to build 6000 edge data centers in a few years. The another path is to develop the edge devices that with computing power and can provide third party applications with open interfaces through upgrading and transformation of industrial field equipment; a typical example is industrial edge gateways. Amazon has released the "AWS Greengrass", edge side software that enables industrial equipment to use AWS cloud services; CASICloud has launched the "Smart IoT", an Industrial IoT gateway product connected to its own INDICS (Industrial Intelligent Cloud System) platform, which can collect, convert, process and transmit data on industrial equipment of different brands and complete functions such as conversion of OT networks and protocols [60, 65].

Since it was formally proposed just a few years ago, edge computing has experienced explosive growth. As such, the edge computing will generate greater spillover effects and become an adhesive for different industries and a catalyst for the Industrial Internet, boosting the upgradation and transformation of the entire industrial ecosystem.

## 4.5  Identifier Resolution

The Industrial Internet identifier resolution system is an integral part of the Industrial Internet network architecture and also the hub that realizes identity management connectivity for the Industrial Internet. At present, the identifier resolution system is still in its infancy and the exploration of innovation in the identifier resolution system is being rolled out gradually. The following innovations have been observed:

1. Research on innovation in open-loop public identifiers and resolution systems

The Identifier system is now mainly applied in such links as asset management and logistics management, and is penetrating into production and manufacturing, for example, machines can automatically read WIP labels to match corresponding processes. With an increase in the demand for product life-cycle management (PLM) and cross-enterprise product information exchange, enterprises' private identifier resolution systems will be integrated with public ones. China's Industrial Internet identifier system architecture is a hierarchical and layered model consisting of root or national top-level and second-level nodes, and provides normative public identifier resolution services for specific industrial applications such as flexible manufacturing and supply chain collaboration, thus enabling closed-loop private identifier and resolution systems to gradually evolve into open-loop public ones. In the future, the employment of either a closed-loop private identifier system or an open-loop public one should rest with whether equipment and work pieces within an enterprise are accessible from outside the enterprise.

2. Research on innovation in heterogeneous and compatible identifier resolution systems

Currently in the Industrial Internet, there are complicated sources of subjects and objects and various forms of identification, which can hardly be unified. Multiple identifier resolution systems, such as Handle, OID and GS1, will co-exist over a certain period of time, thus Industrial Internet identifier resolution systems should be well compatible and extensible. The "integrated solution", based on the basic principle of "openness and integration, unified management, interconnectivity, security and controllability" and relying on national top-level nodes for Industrial Internet identifier resolution, is interconnected externally with root nodes of international identifier resolution systems such as Handle, OID and GS1, and internally with second-level identifier resolution nodes and below that employ different technical solutions and also with the Internet domain name resolution system.

3. Research on innovation in fair and equitable controllable multi-root mechanisms

The traditional Internet governance pattern remains unchanged for a long time and in particular, the independence and fairness of the management of root nodes of the Internet domain name system have long been questioned. Many countries and research institutes are continuously exploring new solutions and governance models. For example, ONS 2.0 already supports consortium root; the Handle technology employs completely parallel cooperation among a number of peer-root, with the data on a root node selectively synchronized to other root nodes and classified data only resolved on that very node.

4. Research on innovation in secure and efficient identifier resolution systems

Domain name identifier coding in the traditional Internet is mainly "human-oriented" to facilitate human to identify and read hosts, computers and websites, while the Industrial Internet identifier coding extends to "be oriented towards human, networks and things" to facilitate computers to automatically read items such as machines, products and raw materials and all relevant information, with much more object data of more types to be identified. Furthermore, the Industrial Internet has higher requirements for network service performance, especially factory internal networks, which require low-latency and highly reliable network services.

Therefore, the Industrial Internet identifier resolution system eases identifier resolution pressure, increases resolution efficiency and upgrades the local resolution latency to millisecond class and the resolution success rate to more than 99% by establishing second-level nodes and public recursive nodes. Compared with the traditional Internet, Industrial Internet involves many key areas concerning national welfare and people's livelihood including manufacturing, and stores more sensitive data, thus limited services or attacks will have significant impacts on the national economy. Industrial Internet identifier resolution can provide a comprehensive security system which guarantees creation, maintenance and management of digital certificates and encrypted channels generated in the operation of the identifier system, data backup, failure recovery and contingent information disaster preparedness for the identifier system, as well as access control of identity authentication and permission management for business processing.

## 4.6   Industrial Intelligence

Industrial intelligence is a technology that, based on data within enterprises, in and across industry chains, integrates intelligent methods into various links such as design, production, management and services to shorten product R&D cycle and guarantee intelligent production, network-based collaboration, personalized customization and service-oriented extension for enterprises. It can greatly expand the boundary of solvable problems in industry circles [66].

Industrial intelligence is in nature information-based computing that substitutes human perception (visual, auditory and tactile senses) and cognition (situation awareness and decision-making), which increases efficiency and precision by applying some algorithms and models and outputs solutions, packages and data packets through cloud and edge computing.

The reference architecture of industrial intelligence is composed of three layers, namely application, technology and deployment, as is shown in Fig. 4.5.

The deployment layer indicates the deployment of industrial intelligence, which is generally divided into cloud (private and public) and edge (equipment) intelligence. The overall system management and security protection are often escrowed by the edge or equipment system in which it is embedded or the Industrial Internet platform of which it is a part.

The technology layer is the core of the implementation of industrial intelligence models and the key to industrial knowledge modeling. The intelligent algorithm framework mainly includes key technologies such as expert system, machine vision, natural language understanding (NLU), robotics, machine learning, intelligent control and data mining.

The application layer embodies smart factory applications involving PLM such as design, production, management and services, and intelligent equipment applications represented by intelligent production equipment and intelligent information terminals.

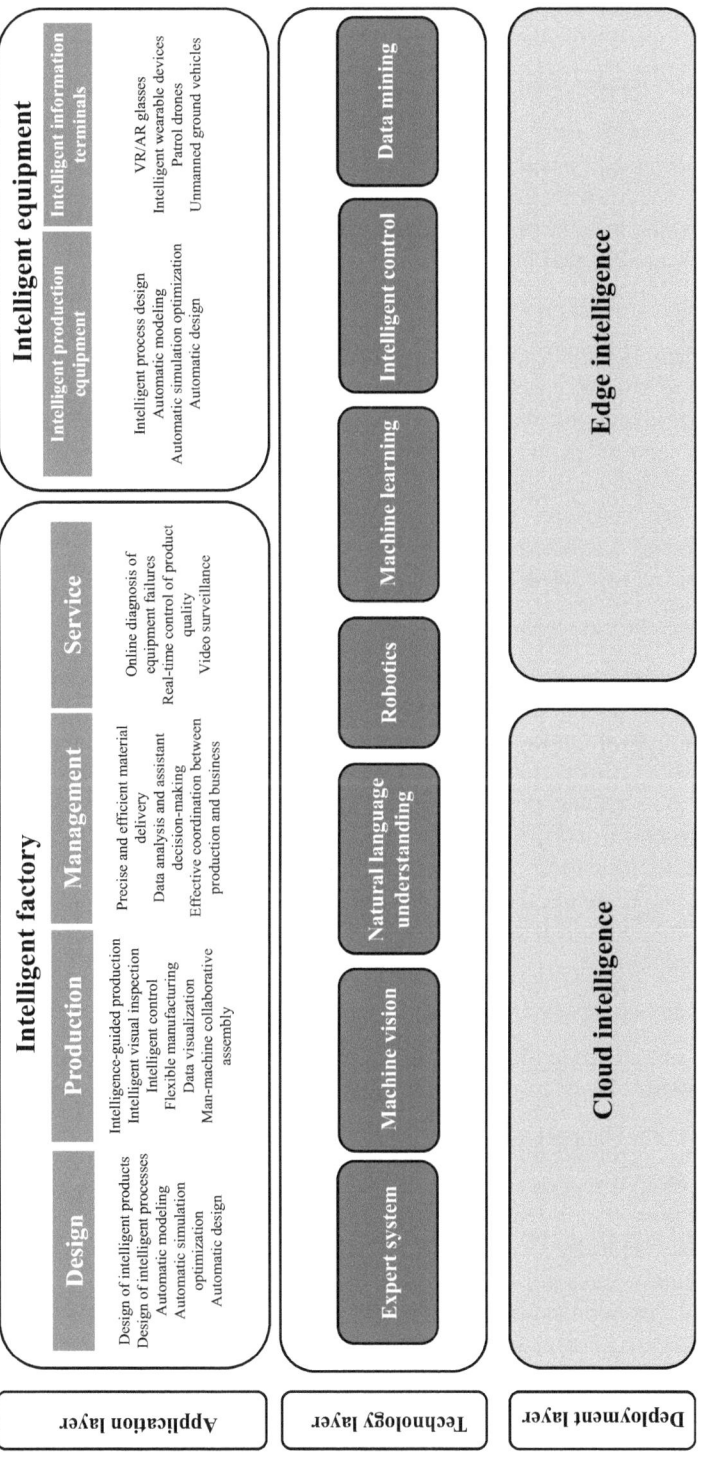

**Fig. 4.5** Reference Architecture of Industrial Intelligence

Applications include the following:

1. Equipment intelligence

Equipment intelligence means that industrial equipment is intelligent and industrial equipment at all levels, from parts, sensors, machine tools to production lines, should be provided with AI to perform self-organizing, self-adaptive, self-executing and self-sensing manufacturing activities, thus increasing the level of intelligence of a factory or a production line.

2. Production and manufacturing process

Throughout the production, different processes should be timely dovetailed with each other to guarantee delivery of products on schedule, during which there are several stages, with orders communicated by personnel from different departments, so the traditional mode has already failed to meet the requirements of increasingly sophisticated operations and high efficiency. In the exploration of higher factory efficiency, many factories are reforming their production processes to make all links transparent and simplified and give fast reactions. Intelligent production is an effective means to solve this problem.

3. Operation and maintenance of production lines

In the production and manufacturing process, high-quality and highly stable operation of production lines is of vital importance to efficient production of high-quality products, but traditional manual inspection is time-consuming, inefficient and expensive. Smart factories definitely can perform automatic production according to individual needs of consumers. Enterprises can monitor the running state and technical indexes of all the equipment on a production line through an Industrial Internet platform in a real-time and efficient manner, and use the big data processing algorithm offered by the platform to precisely locate and predict various working conditions of equipment, give early warning in case of any abnormality and nip it in the bud.

4. Product life-cycle management (PLM)

PLM is a modern corporate management means and its effective management can increase income, lower cost and improve management efficiency for enterprises.

5. Supply chain management

Supply chain management means coordinating internal and external resources of enterprises to meet customer demand. Effective supply chain management will help timely and dynamically respond to customer demand, effectively regulate the inventory and achieve economies of scale [67, 68].

From the development trend perspective, firstly, the computing power of industrial intelligence is evolving from cloud intelligence to ambient intelligence. Due to intelligent computing power limitations, industrial intelligence applications are more found on the cloud. However, industrial production is based on production equipment and production lines and production equipment in industrial production should be monitored and controlled in a real-time manner, which features mass data, high network requirements and valuable information security and privacy. This cannot be met by industrial intelligence services on the cloud and thus requires the capability of providing highly reliable, highly-real-time/quasi-real-time industrial intelligence near a production site to maintain a local intelligent closed loop required by IT and OT integration. Secondly, open-source industrial data training sets and mechanisms for secure exchange of proprietary industrial data begin to emerge, and the access to quality data is the foundation of industrial intelligence. In areas where industrial intelligence applications are relatively mature, such as predictive maintenance of wind power equipment and quality inspection of the steel rolling process through image recognition, open-source industrial data training sets will gradually appear. Meanwhile, in view of manufacturing enterprises' concerns about information security of industrial data, industrial intelligence service providers and industrial data owners show an increasingly urgent demand for secure transmission and exchange of industrial data, and mechanisms supporting secure exchange of industrial data will be gradually improved [69, 70].

## 4.7  Industrial Blockchain

Blockchain is a shared bookkeeping technology, or distributed ledger technology (DLT), based on integrated innovation in a number of technologies such as point-to-point network, cryptography, consensus mechanism and smart contract [71]. Typically, blockchain stores data in a block-chain structure. With a unique trust building mechanism established owing to its features such as decentralization, tampering prevention, transparency and traceability, the blockchain technology is changing the operating rules in many industries and is one of the fundamental technologies for the development of digital economy and the construction of a new trust system in the future [72].

Blockchain enjoys bright prospects for application in industries and can provide trustworthy data storage and exchange for thing-thing interconnection and multi-player collaboration in the Industrial Internet. In practice, preliminary research on domestic and overseas blockchain applications in the Industrial Internet shows that the exploration of relevant applications has just begun and quite a few applications are still in a proof of concept stage [73].

Scenario 1: supply chain management based on Industrial Internet real-time data.

Writing the lifecycle data ranging from raw materials to products onto the blockchain can ensure information on the chain is trustworthy, monitorable and traceable without any third party fiduciaries, helping lower management costs, maintain unobstructed channels of data mutual trust between industrial enterprises and financial institutions, increase financing efficiency and explore new models of industry-finance combination [74].

Industries at home and abroad pay high attention to the huge potential of the blockchain in the field of supply chain management. Internationally, U.S. start-ups like Skuchain have put forward blockchain-based supply chain financing solutions and IBM has announced that it is working with Maersk, a large container transport enterprise in the world, to provide blockchain-based cross-border supply chain solutions. Domestically, Cainiao Logistics has introduced the blockchain technology to increase the traceability of commodities purchased via overseas online shopping while Tencent and CPAG Group have jointly launched a consortium blockchain project—the block supply chain consortium blockchain and cloud ticket platform [75, 76].

Scenario 2: the implementation of distributed IoT in the Industrial Internet.

IoT, as a core function of the Industrial Internet, is designed for comprehensive interconnection between industrial equipment and facilities and products. At present, IoT has a centralized architecture in most cases, which means node data should be uploaded to a centralized platform and corresponding feedback control commands also come from the platform. With the development of the Industrial Internet, industrial machines and equipment, WIP and products will be comprehensively networked, resulting in exponential growth of networked nodes and increasingly frequent node interactions.

If such centralized architecture continues to be used, then centralized IoT platforms will become bottlenecks and distributed IoT will become the development trend [77]. Characteristics of the blockchain, such as decentralization and tampering prevention, provide a new idea for the construction of distributed IoT [78]. Currently, the international community is accelerating the theoretical and practical exploration of the application of the blockchain in the IoT and Industrial Internet. IBM is attempting to combine the blockchain with its IoT platform technology and establish a trustworthy channel for data exchange and sharing between things in the Industrial Internet. In October 2016, the U.S.-based company Chronicled developed a drone delivery system prototype, whereby drones and intelligent locks are authenticated through the blockchain for automatic collection and delivery of goods, thus realizing completely unattended intelligent logistics. In May 2017, SAP released the Leonardo ecosystem, which provides blockchain cloud services, with a view to integrating cutting-edge technologies such as IoT and machine learning [79].

Scenario 3: New Industrial Internet production and manufacturing model based on blockchain.

In the current industrial system, information integration and work coordination between links, including R&D and design, production and manufacturing, marketing and after-sales services can only be completed via centralized platforms and systems, indicating inadequate flexibility of the production organization mode. In the future Industrial Internet system, the demand for small- and multi-batch manufacturing will grow, manufacturing demand and capacity should be dynamically matched on a global scale and network-based collaboration and personalized customization will become typical models [80]. However, how to maintain trustworthy matching between personalized demands and manufacturing resources for supply and demand sides, which distrust each other, on the non-trustworthy Internet remains a major issue yet to be explored in the development of the Industrial Internet. Without any centralized platforms, the blockchain technology can efficiently support collaborative manufacturing worldwide at a low cost. By mapping both supply and demand sides with respect to manufacturing capacity into the participating nodes in the blockchain system, all participants will be able to master supply and demand information in a real-time manner and complete matching between manufacturing demand and manufacturing capacity on a secure and trustworthy platform, thereby laying a solid data foundation for the integration of design, production, management and resource scheduling throughout the chain. The Georgia Institute of Technology has brought forward a blockchain-based Industrial Internet platform (BPIIoT), which can support personalized customization, intelligent diagnosis and maintenance, cloud manufacturing, C2M (customer to manufacturer), and other new models and applications of the Industrial Internet in a distributed environment and enable automation of all processes including order confirmation, manufacturing and logistics.

At present, both the blockchain and the Industrial Internet are in their infancy. Given its characteristics such as tampering prevention, collective maintenance, openness and transparency, the blockchain technology can facilitate the exchange of Industrial Internet data, increase Industrial Internet data security and credibility, lower system construction and operation costs. The combination of the two is expected to generate new business formats and models and should be closely followed. Relevant exploration has begun at home and abroad, and enterprises in the AII have already launched research on blockchain scenarios [81]. In consideration of existing technological bottlenecks, large-scale commercial use of the technology is still some way off and we come up with the following suggestions: firstly, we should conduct some research on blockchain applications in the Industrial Internet. To this end, we should organize systematic research on key issues concerning the application of the blockchain technology in the Industrial Internet, such as relevant theories, technologies, application requirements and scenarios, application models, industrial support environment, standardization, policies and laws, and put forward ideas and the key direction of the promotion work. Secondly, we should explore the experiment of applying the blockchain in the Industrial Internet. In this respect, we should, relying on the AII, select key areas and organize proof of concept, test platform, pilot application demonstration and assessment for the application of the blockchain in the Industrial Internet based on existing practical exploration. What's more, we should provide industrial enterprises with training on blockchain technology and applications in combination with practical experience in pilot and demonstration projects. Thirdly, we should strengthen the research on key blockchain technologies. For this reason, we should carry out the research on core blockchain technologies, product development and integration testing, break through technological bottlenecks in performance, security and compatibility that restrict the development of blockchain applications, support R&D and industrialization of blockchain-related protocols, algorithms, software platforms and applications, develop autonomous open source communities and launch standardization research at due time.

## 4.8   Industrial Internet Security

We should act under the guidance of national strategic plans such as *Made in China 2025*, *National Cyberspace Security Strategy* and *the National 13th Five-Year Plan for Cyber Security*, thoroughly implement the spirit of General Secretary Xi Jinping's important speeches on cyber security and IT development, and advance the implementation of the Cyber Security Law. In the principle of giving play to the major role of enterprises and the supervisory and guiding role of the government and by focusing on equipment, control, network, platform and data security, we should establish an Industrial Internet security protection system with setting up sound systems and mechanisms, enhancing the guarantee system, promoting technological innovation, advancing industrial development and strengthening personnel training as its basic content.

First of all, China should establish a sound Industrial Internet security system and mechanism. China should establish a security responsibility system and standard system for the Industrial Internet in the light of relevant policies and regulations, and gradually refine and perfect its management systems concerning Industrial Internet security. Specific measures may include introducing guidance documents for Industrial Internet security and organizing the formulation of corresponding specifications and guidelines in respect of emergency response, information sharing, data protection and risk assessment. China should establish a security responsibility system featuring enterprises' protection, government regulation and guidance, industrial normalization and self-discipline, and social supervision and co-governance for the Industrial Internet. It should establish sound Industrial Internet security management mechanisms in respect of security supervision and inspection, risk assessment, data protection, information reporting and emergency disposal. China should release guidelines for the construction of a standard system for Industrial Internet security, actively develop a number of badly needed national, industrial and enterprise standards and participate in the formulation of Industrial Internet security standards organized by relevant international organizations.

Secondly, China should step up efforts to establish a technical support system for Industrial Internet security. This technical support system should take into full account the characteristics of security risks in the Industrial Internet and feature coordination at national, local/industrial and enterprise levels. The state should build "a range, a database and a platform", namely a national technical support platform for Industrial Internet security, a basic security resource database and an Industrial Internet network range, and constantly improve the national capability of comprehensively managing and safeguarding Industrial Internet security. Local/industrial authorities should encourage the construction of provincial/industrial technological means and strengthen the alignment with national platforms. Enterprises should be guided to deploy preventive measures, build technological means and enhance their own protection capability.

Thirdly, China should push forward innovation in security technologies, set up national special funds, strengthen its support for innovation in Industrial Internet security technologies and transformation of relevant achievements, make break-throughs in the R&D of relevant core technologies such as identifier resolution security, platform security and industrial big data security, comprehensively increase the investment in R&D and marketing of security products such as attack protection, vulnerability mining, intrusion detection, situation awareness, security audit and trusted chips. Additionally, enterprises should be encouraged to explore ways to improve their own security protection capability by making use new technologies such as AI, big data and blockchain [82, 83].

Fourthly, China should promote the development of the Industrial Internet security industry. It should arouse the enthusiasm of governments, industries, universities, research institutes and enterprises, with the market playing a leading role and the government playing a guiding role. By establishing national cyber security industrial parks, China should integrate industrial resources, develop presentation and market service capabilities in respect of Industrial Internet security and cultivate three to five leading enterprises in Industrial Internet security, which possess outstanding competence in core technologies, strong market competitiveness and wide influence. China should carry out cyber security experiment and demonstration, for example, experiment, demonstration and industrial application of security products and solutions in the field of advanced manufacturing, including integrated circuit and intelligent equipment manufacturing, and promotion of security products, solutions and best practices in industries such as aviation, energy and national defense.

Fifthly, China should intensify the cultivation of Industrial Internet security personnel. It should strengthen publicity and education of Industrial Internet security by delivering speeches in important events such as alliance forums and special sessions and publishing relevant articles via periodicals and journals, WeChat public accounts, websites and other media. China should promote joint personnel cultivation by encourage universities, professional institutions and security enterprises to establish a joint cultivation mechanism, and accelerate the cultivation and selection of compound personnel. China should strengthen training and selection of security personnel, and organize attack & defense exercises and security skill competitions through industry alliances and associations to select Industrial Internet security practitioners at different levels of capacity. China should cultivate high-end security think tanks, gather the information on high-level experts in the industry by relying on national professional institutions and key enterprises, and build technologically leading and renowned high-end think tanks in Industrial Internet security.

# Chapter 5
# Conclusion

The Industrial Internet is not a synonym for the application of the Consumer Internet in enterprises. Although it faces more than a billion netizens, the Consumer Internet is general, while the Industrial Internet is individual for different industries and even for different enterprises in the same industry. The Consumer Internet features few types of terminals, which, with a low threshold for use, are easily popularized and upgraded. The Industrial Internet involves a variety of traditional production equipment, a long business chain and a complex service model, which poses high requirements on infrastructure, technology and security, has a great demand for capital and faces severe personnel challenges due to a serious shortage of personnel not only understanding IT, but also knowing well business processes. The application of the Consumer Internet basically grew out of nothing while the Industrial Internet transforms the existing mode of production and pushes for reengineering, requires changes in industrial organizations. Unlike the winner-take-all pattern in the Consumer Internet, the Industrial Internet needs leading enterprises in more segments and ICT enterprises may play a pioneering role in the physical Industrial Internet, but the dominant role should be left to real economy enterprises [84]. The Consumer Internet focuses on networks, or more exactly, public networks, and adopts a global networking perspective; while the Industrial Internet focuses on enterprise internal networks, which consist of a variety of equipment and IoT at the bottom and usually are not globally networked. So, is it appropriate to design universal identifiers and a new unified resolution system for the Industrial Internet in a similar vein to the Consumer Internet? Some ideas presented in this book are intended to throw a sprat and motivate more innovation practices. In addition, China's Industrial Internet will not develop in a healthy manner unless its industrial automation catches up since all kinds of industrial control software and management software in China are basically imported from other countries.

If the networking problem is solved but that of autonomous controllable software remains unsolved, the original intention of the Industrial Internet cannot be realized. How to connect and integrate underlying industrial equipment into the Industrial Internet is a Gordian knot in the development of the Industrial Internet, which is not

© China Science Publishing & Media Ltd (Science Press) 2020
Chinese Academy of Engineering, *Industrial Internet*,
https://doi.org/10.1007/978-981-15-7490-0_5

deeply discussed here and is expected to be addressed by application practices. In short, the digital transformation of enterprises entails incorporating the Internet thinking into enterprises rather than simply transform enterprises in the Consumer Internet mode, and modifying the existing ICT technology and standards in the light of enterprise demands and then applying the modified ICT technology and standards in enterprises to create greater value added.

# References

1. Wang J. Deepen internet plus advanced manufacturing and develop the industrial internet. Construct Machinery Technol Manag. 2017;30(12):22–4.
2. Zhaoxiong C. The integration of Informatization and industrialization enters a critical period and three types of internet industrial platforms formed, 2017. http://finance.sina.com.cn/chanjing/2017-08-25/doc-ifykiuaz0737966.shtml.
3. Wang G, Yang N, Can C, et al. The latest development and analysis of international industrial internet. Informat Communicat Technol Policy. 2018;10:6–9.
4. Lin D, Shiyang C, Yuze J, et al. Research on key industrial internet security technologies. Informat Communicat Technol Policy. 2018;10:10–3.
5. Alliance of Industrial Internet. Terms and Definitions of the Industrial Internet (Version 1.0), 2019.
6. Alliance of Industrial Internet. Industrial Internet Architecture (Version 1.0), 2017.
7. Alliance of Industrial Internet. White Paper on Industrial Internet Platforms, 2017.
8. Yu S. Advanced stage after industrial internet interconnection: enterprise-AI agent. Study Optical Commun. 2019;1:1–8.
9. Difei L, Nan Y, Ge W, et al. The latest development and analysis of international industrial internet. People's Post and Telecommunications News, October 29, 2018.
10. Xinyi W. New developments and new enlightenments of U.S. industrial internet. Telecommunicat Network Technol. 2017;11:37–9.
11. Lin D. Comprehensively promote security in the industrial internet and other integration areas. Modern Sci Technol Telecommun. 2017;47(6):13–5.
12. Ministry of Economy, Trade and Industry of Japan. The White Paper on Manufacturing Industries, 2018.
13. Qiangdong L. Wages War on Express Companies, Japan to Focus on Investment in the IoT and AI, 2017. https://www.iyiou.com/p/47507.html.
14. Internet Infrastructure Innovation Forum. China internet, 2018.
15. Notice of the General Office of the People's Government of Zhengzhou on Printing and Issuing Zhengzhou Municipal Industrial Internet Development Plan (2018–2025). Gazette of Zhengzhou Municipal People's Government, 2018.
16. Xiaofan L. Wireless technology injects new impetus into industrial internet. People's Post and Telecommunications News, November 1, 2018.
17. Shen B, Lin H. Research on the role of alliances in promoting the development of the industrial internet. Informat Communicat Technol Policy. 2018;7:57–60.
18. Rui H. IPv6 development trend and Prospect. Inf Constr. 2018;6:8–11.

19. Na F, Qingqing W, Jun K, et al. Map matching algorithm for urban road network based on dynamic weight. Measur Control Technol. 2018;37(1):154–8.
20. Technological Developments. Measurement & Control Technology, 2018;37(1):159–62.
21. Hehe L, Tian Z. Development trends of overseas intelligent manufacturing policies. C-Enterprise Management. 2016;6:64–7.
22. Wang B, Lin L, Xiangzhen Y. Research on security of industrial internet. Informat Technol Standard. 2018;10:40–3.
23. Siemens Secures Digital Value Chain through Data Encryption. Security and Informatization. 2017;12:13.
24. Yiyang Z, Wang Y. Interpretation and development of industrial internet policies. Int Econ. 2018;11:34–9.
25. The Guiding Opinions on Deepening the "Internet plus Advanced Manufacturing Industry" and Developing the Industrial Internet Printed and Issued. Indust Control Comput. 2017;30 (12):123.
26. Xiaopeng A. Seize strategic opportunities for the development of industrial internet platforms. People's Post and Telecommunications News, September 25, 2017.
27. Hu H. Industrial internet strides forward and high-quality development makes a good start. 2018. http://wap.cnki.net/touch/web/Newspaper/Article/RMYD201808070011.html.
28. National Leading Group for the Upgrading of the Country's Manufacturing Sector Sets up Industrial Internet Working Group. Secur Informat. 2018;4:8.
29. Zhaoxiong C. Deeply implement the industrial internet innovative development strategy. Administr Reform. 2018;6:17–20.
30. Xiaohui Y, Hengsheng Z, Yan P, et al. Networking architecture and development trend of industrial internet. Eng Sci. 2018;20(4):79–84.
31. Renhui L, Ni Z, Wu Y. Establish industrial internet security protection system to safeguard the development of advanced manufacturing. Informat Technol Netw Secur. 2018;37(1):23–4. 29
32. Rixing C. Internet technology and weighing instrument industry application update. Weighing Apparatus. 2018;47(1):5–14.
33. China's Industrial Economic Development Report 2017, 2018.
34. Yanan Z. CASICloud INDICS industrial internet cloud platform enables manufacturing Enterprises in the Cloud era. Automation Panorama. 2018;3:22–4.
35. Wu J, Youshuang W. Considerations on industrial information security brought by intelligent manufacturing. Informat Technol Netw Secur. 2018;37(3):24–7.
36. Electrical equipment industry planning: policies of 2017. China Electr Equip Industry. 2018;1:22–26.
37. Dig the Essence of Laser Technology to Justify Made in China. Intelligent Manufact, 2017;10:12–14.
38. Yang Z. Capital market speeds up the pace of opening-up and innovation. Financial Times, February 20, 2019.
39. Rende F. Innovative transformation of internet platforms creates a new era for intelligent manufacturing in the rubber industry. China Rubber. 2018;34(1):11–2.
40. Lianru L, Zhongping Z, Li X. Industrial internet of things platform enables construction of industrial ecology. Informat Commun Technol. 2018;12(3):37–43.
41. The Right Time for Industrial Internet Development in Zhejiang. Information Construction, October 15, 2018.
42. China's Cyber Security Milestones in 2017. China Informat Secur. 2018;1:60–63.
43. iTech 2017 Breaks new ground in China's digital economy. Zhongguo Xinxihua. 2018;1:14–39.
44. Wenjuan B. CR: An achievement in localization of high-end equipment manufacturing. China Strateg Emerg Industry. 2018;1:60–1.
45. Evolution of China's Industrial Internet of Things Could Platform Industry. China Indust Informat Technol. 2018;7:58–66.

46. Yifan C. Rankings of the top 100 industrial internet solution providers. China Industry Rev. 2017;9:42–9.
47. Jun H., Xiaohui Y. China's industrial internet platforms are facing three challenges. Machinery & Electronics Business, August 13, 2018.
48. CCSA Sets up the special taskforce on the industrial internet to drive the construction of a manufacturing power. Telecom Eng Technic Standard. 2017;30(8):92.
49. Xiaopeng A. Establish platforms, build ecosystem and promote integration to open a new chapter in industrial cloud development. Zhongguo Xinxihua. 2017;5:8–13.
50. Xin G, Lu L, Luo S. Research on the internet of things-oriented edge computing. Informat Communicat Technol Policy. 2018;7:53–6.
51. Future Trend of the Internet of Things: Edge Computing Is Rising, 2017. https://iot.ofweek.com/2017-01/ART-132214-8420-30098137_2.html.
52. Haifeng H. The influence of the Foundation of the Edge Computing Consortium. Commun World. 2016;33:52–3.
53. CAICT Leads to promote the development of ITU-TSG20 "IoT edge computing" international standards. Telecom Eng Technic Standard. 2018;31(2): 92.
54. Huazhang L, Dan C, Bin F, et al. Standardization Progress and case analysis of edge computing. J Comput Res Develop. 2018;55(3):487–511.
55. Qichao J, Chao R. Research on the edge computing access security system based on a zero trust architecture. Netw Secur Technol Appl. 2018;12:26–7.
56. Xu H. Research on the trend of operators' digital network transformation. Telecommunicat Network Technol. 2018;1:49–52.
57. Weiyang D, Siren C. Build 5G-oriented edge computing. Telecom Eng Technic Standard. 2018;31(4):30–3.
58. Wei L, Wang H, Jie L, et al. Application of WIA-PA technology in metering and monitoring system. Automat Petro-Chem Industry. 2018;54(1):51–3, 71
59. Wu Y. The next technology vent: Edge computing. Secur Informat. 2018;1:21–5.
60. Xiaoguang S., Song L. Pain points, hotspots and drives of industrial internet edge computer. People's Post and Telecommunications News, December 28, 2018.
61. Xueqin J, Hu Y, Yulong X. IoT platform and the open evaluation of its cloud platform. Informat Technol Netw Secur. 2018;37(1):62–4.
62. Tianyi Y. Policies continuously introduced to promote orderly development of "internet+ government services". China Strateg Emerg Industry. 2018;3:32–3.
63. Edge computing to gain popularity in 2017, its value, opportunities and challenges, 2017. http://www.sohu.com/a/124721338_472880.
64. Zhizu L. NB-iot-based urban lighting single-lamp monitoring system design. Electr World. 2018;5:76–8.
65. Zhijie X. Architecture and key technologies of the industrial internet—interpretation of industrial internet: framework and technology. China Mechan Eng. 2018;29(10):1248–59.
66. Analysis of the Profit Model—Intelligent Manufacturing-led Industrial Upgrading, 2018. http://www.360doc.com/content/16/0618/18/16534268_568822717.shtml.
67. Xiang N. Occupy commanding heights in supply chain competition. Brilliance. 2018;3:40–1.
68. Yongnan Z. Research on green supply chain management model—a case study of Quanyou home furnishing. China Manag Informat. 2018;21(19):86–7.
69. Xiangyun X. Research on logistics costs in the context of supply chain management. Da Zhong Tou Zi Zhi Nan (Public Investment Guide). 2018;9:86–97.
70. Donghua H. Research on the influence of big data application on value enhancement of supply chain management. China Comput Commun. 2018;5:140–2. 145
71. Lin S. Blockchain "links" future: reshape the ecosystem in the digital economy era. Journal of the Chinese People's Political Consultative Conference, November 28, 2017.
72. China Academy of Information and Communications Technology. Blockchain White Paper, 2018.

73. Baixue Y, Tao Z, Zongxiang L, et al. Blockchain serves the real economy at a quicker pace. Informat Communicat Technol Policy. 2018;7:42–6.

74. Naifu D. Energy conservation and emission reduction triggers management revolution. Manag Technol SME (Mid-month). 2011;9:78–81.

75. Jianguo Q, Yin Q. Research on product lifecycle management technology. Enterp Reform Manag. 2015;23:38–50.

76. Yongxia J. Tencent registers penguin logistics to participate in business competition, 2018. https://www.pos7.com/38864.html

77. Tang T, Lin T, Wu J, et al. Comprehensive digitalization is the only way to intelligent manufacturing—Interpretation of *Smart Manufacturing System and Practices*. China Mechan Eng. 2018;29(3):366–77.

78. Jiansheng Z. Analysis on the status and trends of patent application of Blockchain Technology in China. China Invention Patent. 2018;15(3):123–8.

79. Yang B, Tao Z, Zongxiang L, et al. Blockchain serves the real economy at a quicker pace. Informat Communicat Technol Policy. 2018;7:42–6.

80. Yan S, Zhen L, Guoyong Z. Security of military data based on Blockchain. J Command Control. 2018;4(3):189–94.

81. Dengguo F, Yonggui O. Preface of special issue on Blockchain technology (Chinese and English). J Cryptologic Res. 2018;5(5):455–7.

82. Gui C. Deconstruct ICO financing: the future of Blockchain digital currency—and analysis of the announcement on preventing ICO financing risks. Inter Finance Law Rev. 2017;4:125–40.

83. Jianrong T, Zhenyu L, Xu J. Intelligent products and equipment led by new-generation artificial intelligence. Eng Sci. 2018;20(4):35–43.

84. Hequan W. Development of "interne+" requires introduction of policies based on Enterprise conditions and establishment of a sound innovation environment, 2018. https://www.mscbsc.com/viewnews-2271344.html.